DEATH…A PRACTICAL GUIDE TO THE CHOICES THAT LIE BEYOND!

DEATH...A PRACTICAL GUIDE TO THE CHOICES THAT LIE BEYOND!

Margaret A. Goralski
Ellen Rusconi-Black
Robert B. Bailey

Writers Club Press
San Jose New York Lincoln Shanghai

Death...A Practical Guide to the
Choices that Lie Beyond!

All Rights Reserved © 2000 by Margaret A. Goralski, Ellen Rusconi-Black,
and Robert B. Bailey

No part of this book may be reproduced or transmitted in any form or by
any means, graphic, electronic, or mechanical, including photocopying,
recording, taping, or by any information storage retrieval system, without
the permission in writing from the publisher.

Writers Club Press
an imprint of iUniverse.com, Inc.

For information address:
iUniverse.com, Inc.
620 North 48th Street, Suite 201
Lincoln, NE 68504-3467
www.iuniverse.com

This publication is designed to provide accurate information on the subject
matter covered. The information provided here is not, and is not intended to
be, professional legal, accounting, medical or psychological advice. You
should consult your attorney, accountant, physician or psychologist with the
specifics of your own situation. Under no circumstances will the publisher
or the authors be responsible for any incorrect or incomplete information
provided here, or for any lost profits or other consequential damages
resulting therefrom.

ISBN: 0-595-13974-4

Printed in the United States of America

Contents

Prologue

This book is written to help all of us better understand the choices that lie beyond. When my sister-in-law, Kathy Grindrod, died an early death, she knew that death was coming and thought that she had made all of the arrangements according to the laws of the land and God. Her choice was to be cremated. She had discussed her decision with my brother, her priest, and the funeral director. She thought that all of the details were clear. When she died, my brother and the funeral director waited 48 hours, which is required by law and then Kathy was cremated. No one had told Kathy, or my brother, that once she was cremated she would not be permitted into the Catholic Church for her own Mass. Her cremains had to remain outside while a Memorial Mass was conducted for her inside, and then we followed her cremains to the cemetery where she was placed in a niche in the wall.

It was just one small omission in knowledge, but my sister-in-law would be angry to think that her cremains had to stay outside of the church, in the car, at her own Mass. I do not want this to happen to anyone else.

Once I began writing, I became more and more intrigued by the Death Care Industry. I have traveled to conferences; visited a variety of cemeteries in the U.S., Europe, and India; and spoken with many interesting people. Jon L. Stephenson, Vice President, and John T. Bailey, CCE and Founder of Mount Olivet Cemetery, Funeral Home, and Garden of Memories; Greenwood Funeral Home and Memorial Park; and Arlington Funeral Home, in Fort Worth, Texas, are two of the interesting people that I have met in my travels. Jon L. Stephenson epitomizes southern hospitality and charm, and John T. Bailey has revolutionized the death care industry by melding funeral homes, cemeteries, mausoleums, showrooms, monument design, and flower services to provide all family arrangements in one single stop. He is truly a remarkable man. Edward Laux, former President of Woodlawn Cemetery in Bronx, NY, is another remarkable man. He gave back to the community in so many ways: by inviting the public to share in the music of "Duke" Ellington and George M. Cohan, who are both interred in the cemetery; and by providing a very special Christmas surprise for the sick children, in Our Lady of Mercy Hospital, who could not travel home for the holiday season.

Margaret A. Goralski

On August 15, 1997 a decree came from Rome, which allows U.S. Bishops to permit funeral Masses in the presence of cremated remains. Each bishop is to determine whether use of the permission is pastorally appropriate in his diocese.

When we began to write this book I had many questions about death and the choices that would be available when my husband Bill dies. Bill and I were in the process of writing our will. I was asking our friend Bob Bailey about cremation: who supplies the urn, how much cremation costs, and if I could lease instead of buy a coffin for the wake. The more that we discussed the options, the more options that presented themselves. Most people we know do not like to discuss death at all. Most are hesitant to discuss the possibilities with their funeral director, and, I myself, noticed that all of the questions that I asked had to do with Bill's death, but, not my own. Margaret and I decided to ask all of the questions, and gather all of the answers, so that you do not have to ask individually. We hope that this book will be as helpful to you as it is to us.

While in the process of writing, my mother, who lived with us, passed away peacefully in the hospital. The experience shed new light on the process of supporting and easing a loved one's journey into death and the myriad of details that follow. One of the greatest gifts that my mother gave to me, as the prime caregiver and executrix of her estate, was her clear and precise, prior to death, preparations. She had clearly laid out her desires in her Living Will, Burial Arrangements, and Last Will and Testament. While facing extremely difficult times, my brother, sister, and I felt confident, and therefore held together to see that our mother, Joyce Rusconi's final wishes were honored. I will be forever grateful to her for her foresight and planning. I feel very strongly that by defining the choices that you wish to lie beyond you are giving the greatest final gift possible to your family.

Ellen Rusconi-Black

The Bailey family have been Funeral Directors for three generations. Robert B. Bailey is the present owner and president of the B.C. Bailey Funeral Home in Wallingford Connecticut. "I hope this book will help people to make decisions with a clear mind. Too often decisions are made while trying to deal with grief." Mr. Bailey sponsored a bereavement group for several years to help people deal with grief.

Robert B. Bailey—Funeral Director and Technical Advisor

Acknowledgements

We would like to thank the very special people who gave most freely of themselves and their time to help us: Mr. Dale J. Fiore of Evergreen Cemetery and Crematory Association—New Haven, CT; Mr. James Shure of Robert Shure Funeral Home—New Haven, CT; Father Michael O'Hara, now deceased, of St. Lawrence Church—Killingworth, CT; Dave Shorrock and Allen Withington, who e-mailed their input from London, England; Christine Whitehouse of Sarasota, Florida; Ponnamma Gopinathan of Kerala, India; and Murale Gopinathan of Haddam, CT. Your candid information, professionalism, and enthusiasm have been essential in the completion of this book.

We would also like to thank the people who read our book, commented, and added their own private observations: Dana Finnegan, Michael Burns, and Ken Whitehouse.

Finally, we would like to thank our families who put up with our continuous talk of death, our discussions of death over dinner, and the continual reviewing and rereading of our book: Joe Goralski, Bill Black, and Darlene Bailey.

1

The Body after Death

He who knows he has enough is rich.
Perseverance is a sign of will power.
He who stays where he is endures.
To die but not to perish is to be eternally present.

Lao-Tzu (604-531 BCE)

During the writing of this book we spoke to many people and two questions have prevailed above all others: why would you write a book about death, and what exactly happens to my body after I die? You know why we decided to write the book from the prologue and what happens to your body will follow.

WHAT HAPPENS TO YOUR BODY AFTER YOU DIE?

It depends on where you are and the circumstances that surround your death. If you die in a hospital, you are usually placed in a pouch and taken to the morgue where the funeral director of choice will pick you up. If you die in your home, the funeral director will come to the house and remove your body on a covered stretcher. If you die in a car accident, and drugs or alcohol is suspected, or, if you die under suspicious circumstances, the state medical examiner for your area will be called and your body will be taken to the medical examiner's office. If the medical examiner is busy, and all of the state medical examiner's cars are out on the road, a funeral director will be asked to pick the body up and will be reimbursed for expenses, by the state, at a later date. The medical examiner visits the hospital every day to examine the bodies of people who have died the day before. No body may be removed by a funeral director without a Doctor's Pronouncement of Death. A Pronouncement of Death is to be issued within 24 hours of death. If there is a nurse in the home, at the time of death, a nurse pronouncement will be made and the Certificate of Death will be signed in the doctor's office the next day.

WHEN DOES RIGOR MORTIS SET IN AND HOW LONG DOES IT LAST?

Rigor mortis sets in 1-12 hours after death and remains for no more than 24 hours. Rigor mortis is the muscular stiffening that follows death.

AUTOPSY

Bob Bailey believes very strongly that you should avoid allowing an autopsy to be performed on a member of your family, if at all possible, but autopsy was one of the decisions that Ellen had to make when her mother was dying and so we will present you with the two sides of the decision and let you think about autopsy on your own and come to your own conclusion. Prior to death the attending physician may speak to you about performing an autopsy on a member of your family after death has occurred. It is an extremely difficult decision to make when someone that you love is lying in the bed and you are trying to come to terms with the impending loss. Ellen's mother's doctor was very sensitive regarding religious beliefs, however, because of the presence of a rare genetic thread that runs from one generation to another, he asked if

Ellen and her family would consider an autopsy, for the benefit of science, when her mother died. Ellen was as reluctant to discuss the topic with her brother as the doctor had been to discuss it with her. Much to her surprise her brother emphatically supported the decision because their family's health history is linked over three generations, all experiencing similar conditions, and Ellen's brother was concerned for his own children. Ellen's mother was a surgical nurse by profession and had spent her whole adult life helping people. This was just one more way to help and so her family agreed. The results were interesting and allowed them to gain more knowledge about their family's health. In some ways the knowledge that they obtained was comforting to them.

When a person dies in a hospital, and an autopsy is agreed upon, the hospital staff will ask a family member to sign a hospital agreement form. There is no charge for an autopsy when it is performed at the hospital. If the body is transported to the funeral home and then an autopsy is selected, there would be charges for the additional transportation and the autopsy itself. Neither of these expenses is covered by insurance once the body has left the hospital.

The funeral home can make all of the arrangements with the hospital and an autopsy will not interfere with your choice to wake, or not wake, with, or without, a viewing.

ORGAN DONATION

Most people don't realize that just having the words organ donor written on their driver's license does not make them an organ donor. If you truly want to be an organ donor, you must notify the organ bank in your area and obtain a donor card. According to the Uniform Anatomical Gift Act, passed in all fifty states, if you complete a uniform donor card you stand the best chance of having your wish fulfilled in any state. If you wish to become an eye donor, you must notify the eye bank, as they have a team of their own that will assure that your eye donation is fulfilled. In addition, if you want to donate your entire body, you must notify the university that accepts bodies in your area.

After you have completed your donor card, you must carry it with you at all times, since it identifies you to medical personnel in case of death.

If you decide to become an organ or tissue donor, it is important that you discuss the decision with your family. It is difficult for family members to make that decision for you when death is near. Usually, consent for organ and tissue donation is asked of the family, or next of kin, even when the donor has signed a uniform donor card. It is, therefore, very important that you have discussed your decision with your family to ensure that your wishes will be met.

If you decide to donate, sign a donor card, and tell your family. Keep the card with you, and if you change your mind, destroy the card, and tell your family. There is no formal registration. Organ donation is a private decision.

There are many types of organs that you can donate. Some are kidneys and pancreas, small bowels, heart, lung, liver, corneas, bones, skin, heart valves, and saphenous veins. A donated kidney can free a recipient from dialysis. A pancreas transplant can keep a diabetic from needing to take daily insulin injections. Small bowel transplants free recipients from needing lifelong intravenous feeding. Heart, lung, and liver transplants can save a life. Corneas can restore lost sight; bone transplants can prevent the need to amputate a limb; donated skin provides temporary covering and protection from pain and infection for burn victims; donated heart valves are used for cardiac reconstructive procedures; and saphenous veins are used in procedures for peripheral vascular disease and as coronary artery bypass grafts.

For more information, contact the Organ Bank 1-800-355-Share.

OTHER DONATIONS

Artificial limbs—Because artificial limbs are so unique to the person to whom they belong, you may think that they are impossible to donate. They can, however, be retrofitted and realigned to be used by another person. You can receive more information about artificial limb donation by contacting your nearest rehabilitation center.

Bodies to Science—If you have decided to donate your body to science, you should keep in mind that after experimentation has been performed, and at some time in the future, the teaching hospital will be done with your body. The usual time frame is approximately three years. If you want your body cremated and returned to your family, or if you want your family to bury you at that time, you should make your wishes known to the organization to which you make your donation, otherwise, you may be cremated with others and placed in an unmarked grave.

2

Funeral Arrangements—The Details

If you don't go to other men's funerals they won't go to yours.
Clarence Day

WHO CONTACTS THE FUNERAL DIRECTOR AT THE TIME OF DEATH?

Both the hospital and the family should notify the funeral director. Usually the hospital will call the funeral home, but some hospitals no longer provide that service. Either way, it is best if the family also calls. It will give you the peace of mind of knowing that your loved one is being taken care of and not lying in the morgue. Even though you may have previously given the hospital information about the funeral home: name, address, and telephone number as part of the medical record; when the time of death occurs it is better for you to make sure that the arrangements have been properly made.

A NOTE ON PERSONAL ITEMS

When a loved one dies in another state or country and has in their possession personal items such as rings or jewelry that are of importance to your family, you can ask that they be sent directly to you by the nurse or doctor in attendance rather than have them travel home with the body. Make a notation for your file of whom you spoke with and what arrangements were made.

BRINGING THE BODY HOME

It does not matter how far or wide a person travels, should death strike a traveler, all you have to do is call your hometown funeral director and he or she can take care of the arrangements. Your funeral director knows the pertinent paperwork that must be filed, how to best transport the body home, and how to maintain diplomatic liaisons with Washington or countries around the globe. It is not the time for you to get involved in international relations, or to try to be understood in a language other than your own. Talk to your funeral director and wait for your loved one to return. **A note of caution**—make sure that you receive, in writing, the expenses involved in the transportation of the body so that there are no hidden fees added after the arrangements have been completed.

TRAVEL TIP

When my mother travels by herself she always gives the travel guide my brother's, and my, fax number at the beginning of her trip. If there are any problems the guide will fax us and we will make the necessary arrangements to bring my mother home or to go and join her. She can travel with peace of mind. If she had a pre-arrangement with a funeral home, they would give her a card to carry with specific instructions for contacting them in case of death.

HOW LONG CAN A BODY BE HELD?

A body can be held for as long as the family wants it to be held, however, it is better if arrangements are made within a week of death.

TO EMBALM OR NOT EMBALM

Except in certain cases, the law does not require embalming. Embalming may be necessary, however, if you select certain funeral arrangements, such as a funeral with viewing. If you do not want embalming, you have the right to choose an arrangement that does not require you to pay for it, such as direct cremation or immediate burial. It is best to let the funeral director know the embalming preference of the deceased as soon after death as possible. If the funeral director holds a body for more than 24 hours it must be refrigerated and a refrigeration storage charge will usually be added. Many Jewish people are not embalmed. It used to be the practice of the Jews to embalm, but the Rabbis of the Talmud objected for two reasons: it was considered to be disrespectful to the dead; and they felt that it retards the swift decomposition of the body, delaying its return to the earth. Embalming is permitted for Jews today if government regulations require it and if the body cannot be buried within three days. However, if a Jewish person is embalmed all blood and all organs (if removed during an autopsy) should be saved in a container and buried in the coffin with the corpse.

WHAT IS EMBALMING?

Embalming is like a blood transfusion without blood. Embalming fluids replace the blood in the body using the same process as a transfusion—one fluid going in—the other coming out. There are many different types of embalming fluid, some reduce the fluid in the body, some puff tissues up and make them look fuller. The combining of embalming fluids to achieve just the right results is an art that funeral directors perform on a daily basis.

HOW DOES A PERSON CHOOSE A FUNERAL HOME?

Most people choose a funeral home that is in the area where the deceased lived for the majority of their life. Other reasons are: they like the way it looks, they like the funeral director, they have been to a wake in that funeral home, or, a friend has referred them. If you are not familiar with any funeral homes in your area, you can contact your local Chamber of Commerce, Better Business Bureau, or Consumer Protection Agency to obtain their recommendations.

WHAT IS THE ROLE OF A FUNERAL DIRECTOR?

A funeral director assists the family through their time of crisis— initially by bringing the deceased person's body to the funeral home, then by securing information for the death certificate to be filed with the proper legal authorities, and then by placing the obituary notice in local newspapers.

The funeral director helps the family make choices, from traditional funeral service and visitation, to a memorial service without the body present, or, even to immediate disposition. Other choices in which a funeral director provides guidance: place, time, clergy person, or other person, to preside at the service. The funeral director will contact fraternal organizations—Knights of Columbus, Masons, Elks, etc. Also, they provide information to help with the choice of casket and burial container, memorial stone or grave marker, and the means of disposition: cremation, burial, or entombment. Your funeral director is knowledgeable about most customs and laws pertaining to death. If there is an item of particular meaning to your family, you should discuss it directly with the funeral director.

On funeral day the funeral director attends to ceremonial and administrative details, as well as the logistics of transportation. In addition, the funeral director helps with claim forms for Social Security, Veteran's and union benefits, and insurance. Because of the emotional impact a death has on a family, the funeral director's assistance during this time is especially important.

Funeral directors are death specialists. They provide guidance and knowledge.

ARE FUNERAL DIRECTORS INTERESTED IN YOUR BODY?

Funeral directors are only interested in your body from a professional perspective. A funeral director is most interested in your face, if there is going to be a viewing. He or she will spend the most time making you look as good as possible.

WHY DO FUNERAL DIRECTORS WEAR A BEEPER?

Funeral directors wear a beeper in case you need to reach them in a hurry.

TO WHAT ORGANIZATIONS DO FUNERAL DIRECTORS BELONG?

- National Funeral Director's Association (NFDA)
- Nation Select Morticians
- Order of the Golden Rule
- and others.

CAN I ASK QUESTIONS?

The people with whom we consulted repeatedly advised that people should ask as many questions as they want. They said that you should feel completely comfortable with your decisions. Purchasing a funeral plan can be a large financial commitment. Prior planning gives you the luxury of time to make the decisions that are right for you and your family.

HOW MUCH CAN YOU CHOOSE?

You can choose the casket and music, but in most states you cannot choose to serve food and drinks in the funeral home and you cannot choose to have soft ambient candlelight. No open flames are allowed in public buildings and no food is allowed in a place where a dead person lies.

BARGAINING FOR CASKETS

Ellen, being a shopper, wanted to know if there was any bargaining allowed for caskets. Bob Bailey, being a professional, after overcoming his surprise at the question, replied that to his knowledge nobody bargains for caskets. I think that he felt that it would be in bad taste. "Caskets come in enough sizes, styles, and materials," said Bob, "that there is a casket to comfortably fit everyone's budget." On the other hand, when I went to help my brother, Tom, to pre-arrange his funeral, we did bargain for a casket and there was flexibility in the pricing. It is one of the best reasons for prearranging a funeral. If you don't like the pricing at one funeral home you can walk away and inquire at another funeral home.

Bob also informed us that there are retail stores that specifically sell caskets. He said that a waiver must be signed before a funeral director will use a casket that a person supplies in case of a defect in craftsmanship. Many casket chains have opened since 1994 when the Federal Trade Commission ruled that funeral homes couldn't charge handling fees on caskets purchased elsewhere. For those who buy their own casket, some discounters hold the sum invested in trust until the customer's death. The FTC rule states that funeral homes can be fined $10,000 for refusing to accept caskets purchased elsewhere. The problem is, at the present time, that two companies—Batesville Casket Co., a subsidiary of Hillenbrand Industries Inc., and York Group Inc.—produce the majority of the 1.9 million caskets sold annually in the U.S. They ship only to licensed funeral directors who are considered to be death-care professionals. This means that companies that funeral directors are unfamiliar with produce the caskets sold in stores. Funeral directors, therefore, do not know the quality of the products that people supply themselves.

CASKET SHOPS

An interesting new trend is the casket shop, which is located in a mall. It is sometimes owned by a prior funeral director, but not always. You can walk into the shop, just like any other shop, look at the caskets and make your burial arrangements or just buy a casket.

WHAT ARE THE DIFFERENCES IN CASKETS?

Although there are a wide variety of caskets, there are primarily two types—hardwood and metal. Hardwood caskets are preferred by some families for their warmth and beauty. They come in mahogany, cherry, walnut, oak, and maple. Hardwood caskets are constructed with the same attention to detail that a master craftsman would give to building fine home furnishings. The prices vary according to thickness and type of wood, design, and grade of interior materials. Some families choose metal caskets for their strength and protection. Bronze and copper will remain durable because the metal will always be non-rusting. All bronze, copper, and stainless steel caskets, and most, but not all, steel caskets are designed to be resistant to the entrance of air, water, and other gravesite substances. A rubber gasket that helps seal the top with the bottom can easily identify protective caskets. Most caskets are factory-tested to ensure that protective standards are met and a full manufacturer's warranty is included with the purchase. The price of a metal casket is determined by type of material, thickness of the material and the design, and the type and grade of interior fabric used in construction. Bronze are in the upper price range, copper is in the middle, and steel is on the lower end. There is also a casket available that is manufactured of pressboard, covered with either a gray material called 'embossed doeskin' or a veneer covering. Caskets made of pressboard are less expensive than those constructed of hardwood or metal.

You can obtain a custom pine, tapered coffin (like the ones seen in the old-fashioned movies) by contacting Rick Webster, Beava Woodworking, Chesterville, Maine.

HOW WIDE IS THE AVERAGE CASKET?

The average casket is 23 inches wide. An oversized casket at 48 inches is available for the full-bodied individual. It may require a special order, but should be available within 24 hours.

JEWISH COFFINS

Most casket companies have specific coffins manufactured for Jewish people. They differ from other caskets in that they are all pegged in wood, have wooden handles, and even the hinges are made of wood. The Holy Burial Society members will usually remove most of the interior stuffing from the bottom of the coffin before placing the body inside. They will leave just a bit of pad for the torso to set on. Jewish law does not require coffins, but if they are used, holes are drilled into the bottom in order to allow the natural process of earth consummation to take place. In Israel there are no coffins. A grave is opened, a bed of reeds is placed in the bottom, and a marble lid is placed upon the body.

THE CASKETS OF PRIESTS AND PUBLIC FIGURES

The caskets of priests and public figures are not hinged, but have a removable lid. This special option allows viewing from both sides. The priest or public figure can lie in state and the parishioners or public can pass on either side. After viewing, the lid clips on.

REMEMBERING THE DETAILS

When you bring clothes for a loved one to wear at their wake bring the same things that you would bring if he or she got caught in a sudden rain storm: underwear, slip, dress or skirt and blouse, scarf if you want, and jewelry for a woman; underwear, shirt, pants, jacket, tie, tie tack, cuff links, rings, and watch for a man. Shoes and socks are optional for both. Make sure that your funeral director knows which items that you would like returned to you. If you want a specific hairstyle, bring a photo. Christine Whitehouse says to bring a current photo, if possible, and to bring the name of the hair dye that was used by the person if you want their roots touched up or their hair colored before the wake. If the person wore glasses and would look odd without them, or if you want glasses tucked in the person's pocket, give them to the funeral director. If the person wore dentures, but took them out before they died, and you want them put back in their mouth, bring them. If the person's hair was not their own, but they always wore a hairpiece, bring it. If a person always wore one particular type of make-up, bring that make-up to the funeral home and it will be applied before viewing hours. In other words, whether artificial limbs, hair, teeth, jewelry, or type of make-up, if it's the thing that made your loved one look unique, the funeral director will do his or her best to include it.

DEATH NOTICES

Local newspapers usually charge approximately $3 to $6 per line for obituaries. Newspaper columns are approximately an inch or two inches wide and a full obituary, written by the deceased as their famous last words, can cost hundreds of dollars. If you would like a laminated copy of the obituary, one that will never yellow with age, it will cost approximately $2.50 per copy. Newspapers have discovered that the creative writing of the deceased is more interesting than the facts only obituaries that were written by journalists in the past, and, it increases the newspaper's income dramatically. If you want your obituary to be correct and you haven't written it yet, perhaps you can include a current biography and a black and white photo (not from your driver's license and not from your high school graduation, unless you just graduated) with your other important papers so that your family will be able to get the facts correct. If you choose to use a photo from the family archives, you can have your local photo store make a perfect copy, usually within minutes, and keep the original for the memorial mass, etc. If you are going to write your own obituary, and you have never been known for your outstanding writing abilities, you might want to get help from a professional writer. May your last words be your best words and may your spelling be correct!

DEATH CERTIFICATES

It can take a week or more to receive certified copies of the death certificate by mail and you will need many of them. If you go directly to the Public Health Department of the municipality in which the death occurred, or to the Town Clerk, you can usually secure certified copies of the death certificate within one day of death. Only certified copies of the death certificate, with the raised seal, are allowed at banks, insurance companies, etc. You need a certified copy of the death certificate for each stock in the deceased's portfolio. The raised seal is most important. No one will accept a death certificate unless the seal is stamped into it.

PHOTOS

If you would like photos of the deceased, or the attendees, it can be arranged through your funeral director or a photography studio, or, you can take photos yourself. Audiocassettes of the sermon, and videos, are also available for members of the family who cannot attend or who would like a memento. All media options should be discussed with the funeral director before the funeral begins.

PRECIOUS PRINTS

Precious prints are the idea of Anthony Kim a designer-goldsmith. A fingerprint impression is taken before burial or cremation by the funeral director and it is made into an elegant oval fingerprint in 14K or 18K solid gold. Call 1-800-KIM-GOLD.

WHAT IS A WAKE?

The term wake actually comes from the Irish practice of watching over the body by candlelight the night before the funeral and, many times, the wild feasting that followed. The practice may have come about because mistakes sometimes happened and a person might not have been truly dead but merely passed out. The wake was to create enough noise to ensure that the deceased was truly dead and to help the mourners forget their grief and resume normal life once they were sure that the corpse was not going to be rising again.

WHAT DO YOU SAY AT A WAKE?

The best thing to say is simply, "I'm sorry." No one wants to hear, "She's better off this way"—or—"I have never seen your father looking better." A simple "sorry" and perhaps a warm remembrance are the best things to say and then move on. Example: "I'm sorry to hear about Mary's death. She was a co-worker of mine at MG Marketing Associates. I will miss her very much." "I'm sorry to hear about John's death. We were best friends in college and, although it has been many years since I have seen him, I'll always remember the way his smile lit up a room."

When visiting a Jewish mourner a guest should not try to express grief with standard phrases, but should allow the mourner to begin conversations about the deceased. You should not change the conversation from talking about the deceased, nor should you use the deceased's name, because to do so would limit the mourner's ability to fully express their grief.

ARE FUNERALS FOR THE LIVING OR THE DEAD?

Although most people will probably say that a funeral is to show respect for the dead, actually, a funeral is more for the living. It is not easy to accept death. It is tough to say good-bye to a loved one. A funeral is the ritual that helps focus our emotions and bring meaning to the experience of death. Rituals designate most of the important events of our life—birth, marriage, death. They denote our link with the past and our passage into the future. The funeral allows mourners to express feelings of sadness and loss and stimulates mourners to talk about the deceased, one of the first steps toward accepting death. The viewing of the body helps us to accept the death and visually shows us that there is no return.

A CELEBRATION OF LIFE

Some people are choosing to celebrate life instead of holding the solemn funeral of the past. When talking with Leslie Steele, she said that her father had two things that he wanted when he died: a solitary bagpiper to play Amazing Grace and a party to mark his passing from this life to the next. She and her family gave him both. Family and friends are not always supportive of people who show respect in an unconventional way. When an acquaintance of my son Chris died, his family sent him on his way with his favorite songs from the Grateful Dead and a celebration of the short life that he had lived—a touch of dank kind buds, a Snodgrass pipe, and a tie-died shirt in which to begin his journey. Recently a friend went to the farewell services of a co-worker's father. There he lay with his favorite things in life—a cigar, a pack of cards, and a bottle of 20-year-old Scotch. Needless to say, there were many amongst the mourners who would have liked to share his Scotch.

GAY FUNERALS

After listening to National Public Radio's segment stating that gay's want the right to be able to die in the way they live, I e-mailed David in London to see what he and his partner Allen thought. This is his response. "From what we've seen from friends who have died from the big A [AIDs] over the last few years, the majority seem to have re-embraced their religious upbringing and the services, either at the church or crematorium, have tended to be relatively traditional. That said, the spin has tended to include a gay clergy, either someone who is openly gay in the Church of England, or a member of the Metropolitan Community Church and orations from close friends or colleagues that explicitly acknowledge the partner of the deceased." So, why has there been a lesser movement away from traditional rituals? David had two suggestions, "The innate conservatism of the British and the camp theatricality of the traditional church service." Although neither David nor Allen had discussed their own funeral wishes with each other, they sometimes discuss where they might like their ashes scattered.

JEWISH FUNERALS

We were fortunate to have Mr. James Shure of Robert Shure Funeral Home in New Haven to help us learn more about Jewish Funerals. He was extremely helpful. A segment of the information he gave us follows. In preparation for burial, the body is thoroughly cleansed and wrapped in a simple, plain, hand-sewn linen shroud. The cleansing of the body is usually done by the Holy Burial Society (Chevra Kadisha) which consists of orthodox people from the community who volunteer to perform this selfless deed for the deceased. It is considered to be the highest act that one can perform because the people involved know that the deceased can never repay them for their kindness. Few know whom the members of the Holy Burial Society are—to know would take away from the specialness of the deed. The fee involved is approximately $100 and is used by the Society for charity, scholarships, etc. The volunteers are usually not paid, however, in some places, like New York City, cleansing of the body is done professionally and the cleanser is paid accordingly. The ritualistic washing is done from head to toe, but the private parts are never uncovered, and the deceased's head is never allowed to drop down during the washing. In death, as in life, there is respect in all things. The last rite the Holy Burial Society performs is to say a prayer to the deceased for any acts of omission. A shroud, called a burial kittel, consists of: trousers, which extend from the abdomen to the soles of the feet and are generally sewn across the bottom of each leg; a slip over blouse with sleeves which are tied at the neck; a coat, which may be either an open-front or a slip-over garment (if the deceased had worn kittel during his lifetime, then that particular garment is used, but all fastening devices must first be removed); a sash, which is wrapped around the kittel three times at the waist and is tied; a prayer shawl (talit), usually the one worn by the deceased in his lifetime; a head covering, resembling a hood, which is drawn over the entire head and neck until it reaches the blouse; a large sheet in which the entire dressed corpse is wrapped. The seven shrouds are used for men; women do not usually use the prayer shawl and often do not use the head covering. The basic requirement is that at least three of the seven pieces are worn. The shroud has no knots. Even the hem is only basted and the threads are left loose so they can be removed. This is to allow that nothing will bind the soul. All parts of the body are covered. There are no pockets and no material goods are taken on the journey, no glasses, and no teeth unless they were in the mouth of the deceased at the time of death, no rings, no jewelry of any kind, nothing that cannot decompose. The Sages decreed that both the dress of the body and the coffin should be simple, so that a poor person would not receive less honor in death than a rich person. A coffin, if chosen, would be a plain pine box in the shape of a mummy, otherwise, all burial containers are called caskets. A proper coffin will be made completely of softwood, will be free of all metal, and will have holes drilled in the bottom to allow natural decomposition to occur. At Robert Shure Funeral Home, we viewed many coffins and caskets made of wood—some simple and some ornate. The casket decision ultimately belongs to the family. According to Jewish law, open casket ceremonies are forbidden and the body is never displayed at funerals. Exposing a body is considered to be disrespectful because it allows not only friends, but also enemies, to view the dead—mocking their state of helplessness. The idea is that just as you wouldn't want someone to look at you while you were sleeping, you also wouldn't want someone to look at you after you were dead.

IS THERE A RIGHT OR WRONG WAY TO CONDUCT A FUNERAL?

No. Funerals are highly personal. Services can be held in a church, funeral home, crematory chapel, backyard, park, or on the shore of an ocean or lake. Music can be as individual as the person who died. Whatever music the person liked in life is appropriate for the funeral service. The funeral home will help you create the best funeral experience for your family. Just tell your funeral director how you would like the funeral conducted.

DO IT YOURSELF FUNERALS

The organization, Funeral and Memorial Societies of America, FAMSA, believes that funerals should once again become a family ritual and that the funeral care industry should not be involved. With 140 Chapters in the U.S. and Canada, they have written instructions on how to care for your own dead and offer advice on local laws and permits on their web site <www.funerals.org/famsa/>. Lisa Carlson is the Executive Director of FAMSA and author of *Caring for the Dead*.

ARE FUNERAL EXPENSES TAX DEDUCTIBLE?

No. Funeral expenses are not tax deductible.

FUNERAL PROCESSIONS

Drive with lights on (low beams). Follow as close as safety and good judgment permit. Approach all intersections with care. Remember that the right of way is given as a courtesy, not a right. Turn lights off at your destination.

The funeral lead car will obey all traffic signals unless directed through by a police officer. If you are in the procession when a light changes or at a busy intersection, you must obey the traffic laws. If you stop you will probably be able to catch up or meet the procession at their destination. If a motorist, having the right of way, gives you the courtesy of letting you pass, you must use your own best judgment before proceeding. When traveling on a highway, the procession will travel close to the posted speed limits. Follow at a safe distance and allow cars to pass through to enter and exit. Everyone might not realize that you are part of a funeral procession if the hearse is not in view. Some people do not know that funeral processions usually stay together. People may think that you own a car with daylights. Since many of the new cars being manufactured have daylights that stay on for safety purposes, it will become more and more difficult to determine who is, and is not, in a funeral procession. Safety is of utmost importance. It would be far worse if you had an accident on the way than if you arrived late or got lost on the way to the cemetery.

CASKET BEARERS

Casket bearers (also know as pallbearers) are a selection of friends, children, or grandchildren who wish to carry the casket of the deceased. They usually volunteer, but sometimes are asked by the next of kin or the funeral director. They are six in number, usually men, but not always. If you do not wish to ask friends or family members, the funeral director has a list of professionals that are available to provide this service. Casket Bearers assist in the movement of the casket in funeral ceremonies, processions, and burial. They do not have to bear as much of the weight as they did in bygone years because church trucks are now available to assist in the moving process. Casket bearers should be evenly distributed. We once watched a funeral where the small men were put at the heaviest end of the casket and all the big body builder types were at the lighter feet section and in the middle of the casket that bears the least weight. They were all family, but the smaller guys were not amused. Casket bearers are usually given a slap on the back, an oral thank you, and a hearty handshake for their services.

CAN YOU HAVE A HOME FUNERAL?

Yes. The body will usually travel to a funeral home for embalming and return to the home for the viewing period, usually followed by a brief funeral service, and a trip to the deceased's final resting place. Before you choose a home funeral, consider the accessibility of the home and the doorway widths. Bob tells the story of a home funeral in which the casket did not fit through the door. No problem, they simply removed the window and slid the casket in, however, it was awkward when all in attendance were waiting and watching from their cars while the casket bearers gently balanced the casket through the window to begin its journey to the cemetery.

FUNERAL SERVICE VS. MEMORIAL SERVICE—WHAT IS THE DIFFERENCE?

A funeral service is held when the body is present, a memorial service is performed when it is not.

TOO MANY FRUIT BASKETS

A family who recently lost a daughter wanted us to note that too many fruit baskets can be a painful experience. They received so many fruit baskets that their home was overrun with fruit flies. It took them forever to clear the air of those fruity pests. The constant swatting at fruit flies, as a reminder of their daughter's death, did not make the mourning experience any easier for them.

WHAT ABOUT FLOWERS?

Funeral flowers are arranged in many different ways, but there are specific types of arrangements that are seen at almost all funerals. A casket spray is usually made of roses and sits like a blanket on the casket lid. It can also be made of carnations and is usually given by a spouse or parent at a cost of $105+. A small heart that sits in the casket is usually given by young children or grandchildren and is most often made up of roses or carnations at a cost of $25+. A standing heart is made with your choice of flowers and is usually given by a close family member. It sits on a stand with the flowers formed into the shape of a heart and is priced at $150+. A fireside basket looks like the basket used to collect flowers, turned sideways with flowers arranged in the front $75+. A spray sits on a stand and the flowers "spray out" in all directions $70+. A large funeral basket and a small basket of flowers are also available for approximately $40+. If purchased in the town of the funeral home to which the flowers are being delivered, there may or may not be a delivery charge, otherwise expect extra charges for FTD service.

WHAT HAPPENS TO THE FLOWERS AFTER THE FUNERAL?

Some flowers are left at the gravesite. Additional flowers remaining after the funeral are delivered to churches, convalescent homes, and hospitals. You may request that flowers be given to an organization of your choice, or you may want to take some flowers home with you. Even if you request that donations, in lieu of flowers, be sent to a designated charity, flowers may arrive at the funeral home.

DONATIONS

Donations to charitable organizations are usually sent directly to the organization. The organization acknowledges the gift with a thank you note to the donor and the family of the deceased is notified of the name of the donor but not the amount of the donation. The family of the deceased should also send a note of appreciation to the donor.

CHURCH MEMORIAL FUND

You can also send a notice that you are donating money to either the deceased's church or a church of your choice in the deceased's name.

MASS CARDS

Mass cards are available for a specific Mass commemorating the birthday of the deceased, the anniversary of the death, etc. They may be obtained at the church in which you would like the person to be remembered during Mass. The offering is usually $5 for a Mass on an unspecified date; $10 for a specific date and time. Mass cards can also be sent to non-Catholic friends, but they may not understand the significance of them.

CLERGY HONORARIUM

A clergy person's fee at a funeral may vary. In the Catholic Church, diocesan law regulates the compensation—which means that it is the same in every parish of the diocese. While some churches may have set fees, others will ask you to give what you feel is appropriate. It is always difficult to know how much is too much and how little is too little. Just go with your gut feeling. The fees can range as high as $150-$300, but, in essence, an honorarium is just that—you decide on the amount and give it. You give at your comfort level.

MUSIC AT A CATHOLIC MASS

Father O'Hara (now deceased) reminded us that a Funeral Mass is not a private affair. It is basically a public Mass, a celebration of the Church, attended by others in the church community. It is offered for the person who has died. Music selection for Mass is confined to the dictates of decency and good liturgy. If your family member had a favorite hymn, it may be fit into the Mass. A singer and the organist are part of the Mass, when available. They are not contracted nor paid separately unless you have made special arrangements.

MUSIC IN OTHER CHURCHES

A funeral service conducted in a church other than Catholic is often a scheduled affair. You can usually choose the music from amongst your family's favorites. You can choose one to two songs. The Minister makes suggestions as to placement in the service and works out the details with the organist and the soloist. It is the choice of the congregation to sing along or not.

THE FAMILY OF THE DECEASED WOULD LIKE YOU TO JOIN THEM

The family of the deceased decides whether or not to have something (breakfast, lunch, snacks) after the funeral; who is going to be invited—family or everyone; where it will be held—home, home of a friend, restaurant or church hall; and who will bring the food—friends, family, or caterer. Usually a kindly friend of the family will go to the place of decision and start the coffee, put out the sandwiches and cold salads, light the oven for hot dishes, and greet guests as they arrive.

THE ETIQUETTE OF ACKNOWLEDGMENT

Written acknowledgments are usually sent within ten days to two weeks following the funeral. They are usually sent for gifts of food, flowers, and memorial fund donations. They are also sent to those who have given exceptional support, as well as to the clergy, casket bearers, and people who provided volunteer services. An oral acknowledgment is sufficient for cards, expressions of sympathy, and telegrams.

WHAT DOES A FUNERAL COST?

Expenses for a typical funeral are between $3000 and $5000. Just the price of a casket, however, can range between $400 and $20,000. The expense for the funeral must be decided exclusively by you. There is no minimum or maximum control on prices of caskets and services, but the Federal Trade Commission states that consumers must be given a complete itemized bill, called a Statement of Funeral Goods and Services Selected, which family members review and sign. You will receive a copy of this document for your file. Your funeral director will usually give you a choice whether you want the church, soloist, musician, and family flowers added to the bill or if you want to make those arrangements separately. For estate purposes, it is sometimes simpler to just have one total bill. This can include donations the family made to the church, certificates, paid newspaper notices, etc.

PROFESSIONAL SERVICE OR BASIC SERVICE FEE

This is a fee of $1000-$2000 that is added to all services and essentially covers overhead. It is the fee charged by a funeral director to act as a general contractor on your behalf. The industry says that the fee is justified because funeral directors are on call 24 hours a day, 365 days a year. Be aware that this fee can be charged even if the funeral director is only receiving an already prepared body, from another state, purely for burial at the point of destination. The Funeral and Memorial Societies of America, a lobbying and educational group, is lobbying to have the fee abolished.

HOW ARE FUNERAL COSTS CALCULATED?

Funeral costs are usually divided into five categories:

- **Funeral home service charges** include: staff, administration, stationery, facilities and equipment, and automotive. Staff is the personnel that are needed to accomplish the service. If an embalming is required, the embalmer will need to spend 3-6 hours preparing the body. By law, a funeral director's supervision is mandatory. Administration fees are for the paperwork that is necessary. When a person dies, the doctor is legally responsible to deliver a Medical Certificate of Death to the funeral director. The funeral director is responsible for completing a government form called a Statement of Death from the information given by the family. The executor, indicating that the information contained is accurate to the best of his or her knowledge, must sign the Statement of Death. These two certificates must then be taken to city hall where the death is registered. The funeral director is then given a Burial Permit that represents permission to bury or cremate the body. When cremation is requested, the Medical Certificate of Death must be taken to a coroner who will investigate the circumstances surrounding the death. When the coroner is satisfied that there will be no further need for medical or legal examination of the body, he or she will give permission to have the body cremated. This permission form is a Coroner's Certificate for Cremation. A Coroner's Certificate for Cremation must be delivered to the crematorium before the cremation can take place. The crematorium is required to keep the certificate on file as a matter of record. The funeral home is also required, by law, to keep detailed records of the information gathered and the activities that take place during the funeral process. Funeral Stationery consists of Memorial Guest Registers, Funeral Announcement Cards, Thank You Cards, etc. Facilities and Equipment is for the rental of the physical building and the equipment needed to carry out the service—bier on which the casket is placed for the visitation and service, a kneeler placed in front of the casket, etc. Automotive includes the use of a service vehicle to transfer the deceased to the funeral home, deliver flowers after the funeral, and to file all of the documents required with government offices. Additional vehicles for the family, casket bearers, etc. are usually available upon request. **Note*** Most funeral homes offer various packages: Direct Disposition, Memorial Service, and Funeral Service that are sometimes the most cost effective way to buy a funeral.

- **Funeral home merchandise** includes caskets or containers, an outer container (burial vault or urn vault), or urn if required. Some funeral homes offer audio visual aids that record some of the activities, like the sermon, for those relatives that may not be able to attend.

- **Cash advanced**—In order to consolidate the accounts incurred by a funeral, the funeral home usually offers to pay for items such as cemetery expenses, newspaper notices, clergy honorariums, etc. This service helps in the orderly management of the estate. These charges are not made by the funeral home nor does the funeral home profit by them, but they are funeral related and usually added to the funeral account.

- **Goods and services tax**
- **Other** allows for particular requirements of a particular funeral (shipment of the body, transfers from the airport, long distance telephone calls).

DO YOU REALLY HAVE A JOINT ACCOUNT WITH THE DECEASED?

It is always best to double check. Over the years, Ellen had signed numerous bank signature cards for her mother. When her mother became ill and it was difficult for her to sign, Ellen signed the checks in her own name thinking that she was a joint account holder on the checking account. To Ellen's great surprise, she discovered, after writing the check for her mother's funeral, that she was not a joint signatory. The issue was quickly remedied and Ellen was appointed Executrix by the Probate Court.

3

Pre-Arranging Funerals

WHAT IS A REVOCABLE FUNERAL CONTRACT?

A revocable funeral contract **can be canceled** at any time or changed to another funeral home and most of the money will be returned. There is no limit to the amount of money that you can put aside for funeral arrangements, however, any amount over the $5,400 allowed by the State (this amount is for Connecticut) will be lost if the person goes into a Title XIX program. Title XIX, or State Medical Assistance, is a health care program operated by the Department of Income Maintenance, like Medicaid.

WHAT IS AN IRREVOCABLE FUNERAL CONTRACT?

An irrevocable funeral contract, in the State of Connecticut, for example, can be set up for a maximum of $5,400 (at the time of this writing). You should check into the amount that is allowed in your State. This contract is protected from the State for that amount of money if a person goes into a Title XIX program. An irrevocable funeral contract **cannot be canceled,** but it can be moved to another funeral home.

A 5% handling charge can be added by the funeral director to either a revocable or an irrevocable pre-need funeral contract in the case of cancellation or movement.

QUESTIONS TO ASK BEFORE YOU ARRANGE FOR A PRE-NEED PLAN

- How will the funds be invested?
- What happens to the interest earned on my investment?
- What happens if the funeral home goes out of business?
- Will the agreement be honored if I die before the plan is fully paid?
- If not, will my family be responsible for the payment in full?
- Does pre-payment freeze the cost of funeral goods and services?

ARE THERE OTHER WAYS TO FUND A FUNERAL IN ADVANCE?

Yes. You can earmark an insurance policy, trust, or special bank account for this purpose. These ensure that your funds are guaranteed, plus you earn interest.

KEEPING THE FAMILY IN MIND

When pre-arranging a funeral, keep in mind the needs of your family members. When my sister-in-law, Kathy, was dying, she and my brother had discussed the funeral arrangements that they felt would be best for their family. They thought that her death would be painful enough for their young adult children without having them go through the trauma of standing and greeting people at a wake. After Kathy died and there was no wake, just cremation and a Memorial Mass, some of their children felt deprived of the opportunity to say their final good-bye to their mother. They would have liked the support of extended family and friends to make the passing a bit easier, to discuss their mother and her attributes with others, and to laugh at the good times that they had shared.

FOR ADDITIONAL INFORMATION

Most states have a licensing board that regulates the funeral industry. You may contact the licensing board in your state for information or help.

PRE-ARRANGING A FUNERAL

You can pre-arrange a funeral by completing the following form and discussing it with your family. It allows you to take your time, think carefully, and make the arrangements that are best for you. Once arrangements have been made, ask your funeral director for an ID card to be kept with you at all times. At the time of death, he or she will be contacted directly. Add your Hebrew name and dates, if needed.

PRE-ARRANGEMENT FORM

1. Full name: _____

2. Maiden name: _____

3. Date & place of birth: _____

4. Names of parents: (addresses and phone numbers if living) (full names—include maiden name of mother and birthplace)

    _____

    _____

    _____

    _____

5. Social Security Number: _____

6. Resident of town since (yr.)_____In State since (yr.)_____In the USA since (yr.)_____

7. Name & address of spouse: _____

    _____

    _____

8. Date & place of marriage: _____
    Marital status: single married divorced widowed

9. Names & addresses of any previous spouses:

    _____

    _____

    _____

10. Names, addresses, and phone numbers of children:

    _____

    _____

    _____

    _____

    _____

11. Names, addresses, & phone numbers of brothers & sisters:

_____

_____

_____

_____

12. Names, addresses, & phone numbers of other friends and relatives who should be notified:

_____

_____

_____

_____

_____

_____

_____

13. Names & addresses of present & previous employers:

_____

_____

_____

_____

_____

_____

14. If you are a veteran:
   - date & place of enlistment: _____
   - date & place of discharge: _____
   - rank & service number: _____
   - organization or outfit: _____
   - commendations received: _____

   _____

- location of discharge papers: _____
- flag desired to drape casket: _____

15. Religious affiliation: _____

16. Professional & fraternal organization memberships:

    _____

    _____

    _____

    _____

17. Do you wish a fraternal order to participate in the service, if so, which one?

    _____

18. Education (list schools attended and dates of any degrees or honors received)

    _____

    _____

    _____

    _____

19. Names of newspapers in which you would like your obituary to appear:

    _____

    _____

    _____

20. Organ donation (list of authorized cards and anyone who should be notified):

    _____

    _____

    _____

21. Funeral director or funeral home that you prefer:

    _____

22. Do you have a pre-arranged funeral contract? If so, location of contract:

_____

23. Clergy person or anyone else who you would like to offici-ate:_____

24. Do you want a viewing time for family & friends?

_____

25. Do you want a private viewing for family only?_____
26. Do you want a full wake for family & friends? _____
27. Music, hymns, or readings that you would prefer during your service:

(You may attach this material, if available.)

_____
_____
_____

28. Memorial gifts in lieu of flowers? _____
29. To which organizations would you like donations made in your memoriam?

_____
_____

30. Names, addresses, & phone numbers of casket bearers:

_____
_____
_____
_____
_____
_____

31. Name, address, and location of cemetery property (include lot and grave number):

_____

_____

32. Type of grave marker and inscription desired:

_____

_____

33. Casket and/or vault preference: _____

34. If you wish to be cremated, include disposition preference:

_____

35. Do you wish immediate burial or cremation, with a memorial service in the church or synagogue afterwards? _____

36. What is your desire about the cost of your funeral? _____

37. What are your favorite flowers and what colors do you like?

_____

38. Exact location of your will: _____

39. Who is the executor of your will? Name, address, & phone:

_____

_____

40. Location of safe deposit box and key: _____

41. Attorney's name, address, & phone number:

_____

_____

42. Location of checking accounts, checkbooks, savings accounts:

_____

_____

_____

_____

_____

43. Credit cards and charge accounts to be cancelled:

_____

_____

_____

_____

_____

44. Location of insurance policies:

_____

_____

45. Any additional instructions:

_____

_____

_____

_____

_____

Please include or attach any special photographs, or mementos that you would like included.

4

Cremation

Indira Gandhi was cremated on 3 November 1984.
There were no blue flames in the fire that leaped toward
the setting sun, red, saffron, and gold were her colors
and saffron and gold were the flames.

Pupul Jayaka
An Intimate Biography—Indira Gandhi

CREMATION

Cremation began during the early Stone Age, approximately 3000 BCE. During the Bronze Age 2500 to 1000 BCE, cremation expanded from its origins in Europe and the Near East into the British Isles, Spain, Portugal, Hungary, and Italy. Around 1000 BCE cremation became more popular in Grecian customs and by 800 BCE it was the recommended choice for slain warriors. By the year 600 BCE, it is believed that the practice of cremation had moved to the Roman Empire with cremains being stored in elaborate urns. Cremation was not popular with the Christians. In 400 AD, with Constantine's Christianization of the Empire, earth burials replaced cremation, except during war and plague, for the next 1500 years. Modern cremation began a little over a century ago after Professor Brunetti perfected his cremation chamber.

RETORT

Retort is the name of the machine that performs the actual cremation. It operates at 1500—1900 degrees. Low capacity retorts take approximately 3 hours; high capacity machines take less than an hour depending on the type of retort, size of the individual, and the number of cremations in a day.

DIRECT CREMATION

Direct cremation is the immediate cremation and disposition of the body with no attendant rites or ceremonies.

CREMATION AND THE MEDICAL EXAMINER

A Medical Examiner must examine any individual that wishes to be cremated. The person must be checked for physical appearance to make sure that there has been no foul play. The color of the eyes, teeth or dentures (according to dental charts), scars, height, and weight will be noted to assure that the person to be cremated is actually the person who is designated as the corpse. Once cremated, there is no second chance. No person shall be cremated until 48 hours after death.

CASKET RENTAL

If you wish to have a viewing, in many states caskets can be rented, however, not all funeral homes will have caskets for rent. The casket rental price can range from $395 to $995. Every funeral home determines its own price. In a rental situation, the body may be placed in a regular casket and the funeral director will change the interior, or, a casket may be used with a removable shell interior that then becomes the cremation casket.

CREMATION CASKETS—ETC

Another option is to purchase a cremation casket that can be used for the wake and then cremated. Cremation caskets are made of materials like fiberboard and give the appearance of wood at a fraction of the cost. In some states it is not required that a body be cremated in a casket. In such cases a simple cardboard container or pouch will be used. The cremation container or casket should be strong enough to assure the protection, and the health and safety, of the crematory operator, and it should provide a proper covering for the body and meet reasonable standards of respect and dignity. If you have chosen a metal casket for the funeral service, the body must be transferred to an acceptable cremation container after the service and prior to cremation.

WHAT IS CREMATION?

Cremation is a process of extreme dehydration and evaporation created by intense heat which reduces the composition of the body to bone fragments. The fragments are then processed into a substance called cremated remains, human remains, or cremains.

THE PROCESS OF CREMATION

The body is placed in a cremation container and put into the cremation chamber. Using heat of approximately 1700 degrees, the body is reduced to bone fragments through extreme dehydration and evaporation. After a cooling period, the cremains are removed from the retort and non-combustible materials are removed. The bone fragments are then processed and placed in either an urn or a temporary container.

IDENTIFICATION OF CREMAINS

When a body is put into the cremation chamber, a metal tag with a number, and crematory identification, is put next to the chamber door and follows the person through all stages of cremation until the tag is placed into the urn of the person that has been cremated.

CREMAINS

After completion, the result of the cremation process has neither the appearance, nor the chemical properties of ashes. The cremains, or cremated remains, are bone fragments. These elements are either placed into a permanent urn, or into a temporary container that is suitable for transport if the cremains are to be scattered. Depending on the size of the body, the cremains usually consist of three to nine pounds of bone fragments. Some crematories process the cremains to reduce the space they require. Others do not alter the condition of the cremains after they are removed from the cremation chamber. If the condition of the cremains is important to you, you should discuss the final result with your funeral director or crematorium supervisor before the process begins. There are usually three final forms of cremains: bone fragment, pellets, or completely pulverized and ash like. The color of the cremains is the same whether the body has been embalmed or not. The cremains are a pale off white gray. The only thing that changes the color of cremains is the container in which the body is cremated. Some hardwood caskets will change the color slightly. Connecticut law states that the cremains must be non-recognizable bone fragments of less than 1/2" in size. This may vary from state to state. It is best to check with your funeral director or director of crematory services. After cremation, all metal pieces are removed from the bone fragments by running a magnet over the remains. Assorted metal pieces are from the casket, such as nails and decorations, and from implants used to repair various injuries. Cremation does, in a portion of a day, what it takes 200 years to occur naturally.

CREMATION OF PORTIONS

Some people, who have had limbs amputated, have the amputated portion cremated and held until the time when the rest of their body will be cremated. At that time the cremains are combined to create the whole.

PACEMAKERS AND CREMATION

A pacemaker, or any type of battery—hearing aid, etc. will be removed by the funeral director before cremation occurs, otherwise, it may become dangerous when subjected to the extreme heat of the cremation chamber. Lithium batteries explode in the retort, like a firecracker, and could cause damage to the operator and the tiles of the retort.

CREMATION & INFECTIOUS DISEASE

When a person with an infectious disease dies, that person is tagged with a red toe tag before the body is transported to a funeral director. Crematory operators, and funeral directors, take special precautions when they are informed that a person has died of an infectious disease and universal health precautions are employed. Gloves will be used to move the cremation casket, a mask will be worn, and windows and doors will be left open to allow better air circulation for the crematory operator. Bodies that have been embalmed would cause less risk for the crematory operator, but more risk for the funeral director.

TIME INVOLVED IN CREMATION

The retort takes approximately an hour to heat, cremation takes between 2-4 hours, and the unit takes approximately one and a one-half hours to cool down enough for the operator to remove the cremains.

Cremains are shipped to the funeral director from which they came for return to the family, or a friend of the deceased.

IS THERE AN ODOR AROUND A CREMATORY?

No. Retorts burn at such a high temperature that there is not usually an odor around a crematory, and, some crematories have a re-burn exhaust so that no smoke is released up the chimney either.

WHAT TO DO WITH CREMAINS

Inurnment is the containment of the remains in an urn. The urn may then be placed in a niche at a columbarium, buried with a memorial stone or in an urn garden, set in a place of respect, scattered, or taken for a ride.

A columbarium was originally a dovecote or a place where the doves came home to roost. Modern funeral directors gave the name to a building with little niches in the wall for urns holding cremains. Glass doors, or other barriers, prevent pigeons from coming home to roost in these present day columbariums. Columbariums can be found inside and outside.

Another alternative is to bury the cremains in a grave with a memorial stone. According to our source, you can only bury two urns of cremains to a lot, but check with your cemetery for specifics because some cemeteries allow you to bury many more.

Special urn gardens (an area set aside for the burial of urns) are also available in some churchyards and cemeteries, or you may choose a special memorialization such as a tree, rose bush, or perennial plant.

Some people like to place the urn within their home, on a mantle or other place of respect, and some families choose to have the remains scattered in a favorite place. It is not legal to scatter cremains in all locations. You can ask your funeral director for advice about restrictions in your area.

And finally, some people just leave the cremains in an urn in their trunk to ride around with them and share their life on a daily basis.

Sometimes, like when a person begins dating after a loved one has died, having the cremains of a past spouse becomes embarrassing and somewhat disrespectful. At that time you might want to contact your church or a local cemetery and make a decision about locating a final resting-place.

URNS

An urn is a sealed container used for holding cremains. It comes in a large variety of styles, designs, and materials. There are basically five types of urns: cast bronze, which is the highest quality 100% solid sculptural bronze, takes 2-4 weeks to complete, has extensive hand-work, is considered artwork for the home, and is naturally non-rusting and durable; sand-cast bronze process is of highest quality 100% solid bronze, has a seamed case bronze construction, and is naturally non-rusting and durable; solid hardwood comes in a wide variety of premium hardwoods in a variety of styles and has a rich hand finish; solid marble or granite is hand-crafted from solid blocks of semiprecious marble or granite in a variety of colors and patterns that make each urn an original, and offers the durability of stone; sheet metal comes in a square or rectangular shape, is a non-rusting material, and has the durability and lasting quality of bronze at a lower price.

The cremated remains of an average size adult need to be stored in an urn that has a capacity of at least 205 cubic inches, which is slightly less than the size of a gallon jug. Any shape, size, or design of urn is okay, however, some niches have size requirements. You may provide your own urn of special significance to you or your family, or, you may transfer the cremains into another container at a future date.

Keepsakes may be placed within the urn with the cremains, but, keep in mind the size of the container and tell your funeral director of your intention before cremation begins. You may want to ask your funeral director if he or she stocks urns, or if the funeral home purchases urns from a catalog. You may also ask how long it will take to obtain the urn. This may reflect on your arrangements for placement of the urn, and scheduling, if family members and friends plan to be present. Furthermore, you may wish to let your funeral director know if you prefer to have the funeral home hold the cremains until placement is scheduled or if you would prefer to bring the cremains home as soon as possible. There are also smaller urns available for the cremains of babies or children.

Crematories usually put cremains in a temporary container.

KEEPSAKE URNS

Keepsake urns are smaller and have been created to use as a keepsake in the home. They are designed to hold only a portion of the cremains, for memorialization, when scattering is chosen. These smaller urns can be used to divide cremains among family members and friends, or as gift mementos. We have found during the writing of this book that many changes are forthcoming both in items and materials available to your family to use as vessels for cremains. Many funeral homes are rather conservative establishments and if you want something unique or different do not hesitate to ask. We found that some Funeral Directors did not know about keepsake urns or cremation jewelry, but if you ask, they will find them for you.

CREMATION JEWELRY

If you want to keep your deceased relative close to your heart, you can purchase pendants in many designs, which have a locket-style compartment for storing cremains. The pendants are available in heart, teardrop, and cylindrical shapes and are approximately the same size as other lockets.

SHIPMENT OF CREMAINS

At the time of this writing UPS would not ship cremated remains; however, the U.S. Postal Service is very accommodating.

THE SCATTERING OF CREMAINS

Give considerable thought before scattering cremains. Emptying an urn of all that remains of the person you love can be a traumatic experience. Keep in mind that, like ashes in the wind, cremains will blow into your face, eyes, and mouth if you release them on a windy day. Pick the day well, and stand to the side.

MEMORIALIZATION

Some families feel that the cremated remains of someone they love should be given a place that can be identified with a name and important dates. This is called memorialization. This special place serves the family's basic need of remembering and being remembered. Some cemeteries and churches have scatter gardens that provide a tangible place to visit your deceased family member and a special memorial wall for identification.

UNCLAIMED CREMAINS

When you decide that cremation is the desired choice for you; you should also decide how you would like your cremains to be disposed. When we spoke with Dale J. Fiore of Evergreen Cemetery and Crematory, he said that sometimes cremains are not collected from funeral directors. At first I found this information to be astounding. Who would not collect the cremains of a family member? Dale explained that sometimes a person chooses to be cremated and the family fulfills that choice, but they do not wish to have the cremains of their daughter, spouse, or father sitting on the mantle, or in the trunk of their car, and they do not know what to do with the cremains. Almost every funeral home has a shelf of unclaimed cremains. Before you die, decide exactly what you want done with your cremains and discuss it with a person who will carry out your wishes, otherwise, you might be left on the shelf of a stranger.

WHAT DOES CREMATION COST?

The cost of cremation, when provided through a funeral home, averages between $1500 and $2000, with additional services, $2500 to $3500 is more common. Cost for direct cremation (check the yellow pages) is approximately $800-$1000. Through cremation societies the cost is approximately $450—$1050 (see death alternatives section).

CAN YOU PRE-ARRANGE CREMATION?

Yes, you can prearrange cremation through a funeral director, direct cremation service, or a cremation society.

USE OF THE CHAPEL

Some crematories have a chapel on site that can be used if you desire. There is usually a charge associated with the use of the chapel of approximately $100 per hour. If you wish to have music, you may have to bring your own records, tapes, or CDs and something to play them on. If you wish to have someone speak of your grand accomplishments in life, you or a family member will have to arrange it with the person of your choice. Check with your funeral director or the crematory operator about what is, and is not, available before you arrive.

CREMATION AND THE CHURCH

The Catholic Church has accepted cremation since 1963, however, the Church does encourage that Catholic Funeral Rites be carried out prior to the cremation taking place and that anyone choosing cremation should wait until after the Funeral Mass. After the Mass, the Church states that the cremains should be treated with respect and be entombed in a mausoleum or columbarium. The practice of scattering cremated remains on the sea, from the air, or on the ground, or keeping cremains in the home of a relative or friend of the deceased is not the reverent disposition that the Catholic Church requires. When cremated remains are present at a Funeral Mass, the instructions for the liturgy states that the remains are to be contained in a "worthy vessel" and placed on a table or stand where the casket would normally be positioned.

The Protestant Church has supported the idea of cremation for decades. Baptists, Church of God, Mormons, and other Christian groups, while not prohibiting it, do not encourage it. In all religions there are regional differences, so check with your clergy first.

According to Jewish law the body must not be cremated; the body must be buried in the earth, but that does not mean that some Jewish people are not cremated. An observant Jew will be buried and allow natural decomposition to occur, but some feel that their body has turned on them through a ravaging disease or through time, and under those circumstances cremation might be chosen.

TRENDS AFFECTING CREMATION

A greater number of people are choosing cremation today for a number of reasons. Some reasons stated in a recent study include: an increase in the age of the deceased, the widespread migration of families, the greater acceptance of cremation as a viable choice, the limited amount of space available for burial, and environmental issues. The largest single deciding factor in choosing cremation is monetary.

5

The Cemetery

"A place of great natural beauty can heal the bereaved and
give their descendants a welcoming and comforting place to
which to return to remember and commemorate
those who have gone before."
Founders of Mount Auburn Cemetery in the year 1830

CHOICE OF CEMETERY

A cemetery is usually chosen based on its religious affiliation. People
from one religion will not normally be buried in a cemetery of another
religion, nor, usually, can they be. After religion, the next priority is the
upkeep of the grounds. Visiting many cemeteries in your area will allow
you to determine the overall appearance, amount of sun or shade, trees
or grass, etc. Most people want to be close to their family, so nearness to
family and friends is another factor. And last, but not least, is the type of
monument that is allowed, or restricted, in the cemetery of your choice.

BRIEF HISTORY

Neanderthals began to bury their dead at some time between 20,000 and 75,000 years ago and people have buried their dead ever since. In the past, because of a burial ground's potential for spreading disease, many cemeteries were placed outside of the city proper. Church burial grounds were highly popular places and there was not always enough space available, therefore, people were buried on top of each other, over and over, to make room for additional layers. The practice of selling the same grave more than once was begun by church sextons who were faced with a large demand and limited space.

In the 1800s, in the United States, garden cemeteries were created that were not associated with any particular church or parish. Mount Auburn Cemetery in Cambridge, Massachusetts was the first, and is still one of the most beautiful. The decision to change cemetery design was based on the romanticism of death, together with a series of devastating epidemics. The public loved these new garden-variety cemeteries with trees of many species and often walked amongst the monuments with their families on a Sunday afternoon. Many of the most impressive parks in the United States, that were created during and since the 1800s, were based on the popularity of these original garden cemeteries.

CASKET ALARMS

Old trade journals carried advertisements for casket alarms. In today's world, medical science has progressed to the point that we are now fairly certain if a person is dead, or not, when they are buried in the ground. It is, therefore, now believed that a casket alarm is no longer necessary, however, this is the way that it worked: when a person was put into the casket, a casket alarm was installed; if the person should wake up, and find themselves lying in a casket, they would ring the bell. The cemetery watchman would hear the bell ringing and the person would quickly be dug up. Our personal opinion is that the cemetery watchman would probably run for the nearest gate.

EARTH BURIAL OR INTERMENT

An earth burial or interment is the most common form of disposition of the body in the United States. U.S. citizens seem to prefer the idea of a final resting place and a gravesite where family members can visit.

TO LOWER OR NOT TO LOWER?

One of the most difficult things for a family, is to watch a loved one being lowered into the ground. Most people prefer to leave the cemetery while the casket sits on top of the earth to be lowered by cemetery employees at a later time. It is important to some Jewish people, the Amish, and gypsies to bury their own dead by lowering the casket into the ground and by tossing earth onto the casket. There is a distinct sense of closure when earth hits the lid of a casket. The sound signifies finality. Hispanics participate until the casket is lowered into the ground, flowers are tossed in, and the vault cover is put in place. Some Orders of Masons each throw three shovels full of dirt onto the vault before their ceremony is complete. To lower or not to lower is a decision that each family must make based on their own tradition and ability to cope.

BURIAL IN A PLAIN PINE BOX

Burial is allowed in a plain pine box, but most cemeteries demand that it be placed within a liner, not to protect the dead, but to protect the living, otherwise, while walking through a cemetery, if the pine box is at the stage when the top has rotted away, the living could well find themselves falling into the land of the dead.

CAN YOU BURY A LOVED ONE IN A BACKYARD CEMETERY?

You cannot bury a loved one in a backyard cemetery unless it is a pre-existing family cemetery.

FAMILY MEMORIALS—MARKERS & MONUMENTS

Most families choose some form of marker or monument to memorialize the deceased. Markers vary from large granite or marble memorials to small bronze plaques. Some families that choose cremation, and scatter the cremains, also purchase space in a cemetery, or church, for an inscribed memorial plaque. There are basically two types of markers, upright memorials and flat memorials.

Upright memorials stand up from the ground anywhere from a few inches to many feet in height and come in many sizes. They can be made of marble, granite, many types of stone, cement, bronze, and throughout history, wood. Some cemeteries have restrictions on what type of marker may be used in a particular location, and the restrictions may change from section to section.

Flat memorials are set in place to be level with the ground for mowing and ground maintenance purposes. Bronze and granite are the preferred marker materials, granite because it comes in many different colors. The usual sizes are 12" x 24" or 16" x 28" although the size may vary depending on the cemetery.

Markers come in many designs and styles. At this time the sky is the limit. If you can create it in your mind, you can have it etched in stone and placed upon your grave marker. If you need more space than a grave marker can provide, there is a new monument by Living Monuments that has a stone cylinder set within the monument on which you can have your life story engraved. Visitors just spin the wheel and the story that you wish to tell is set before them.

When you have chosen a cemetery, you should look at the markers that have already been set in place to get a feeling for the surrounding area. Choose a monument well. It will represent you and your family for an eternity.

HOW LONG DOES IT TAKE TO ERECT A MONUMENT?

In New England it takes an average of 6-8 weeks to complete and install a monument depending on materials, design details, weather, and ground conditions. Most cemeteries have specific guidelines on the foundation requirements, size, and type of marker or monument that can be erected. Before purchasing a monument, a cemetery lot should be purchased and the memorial guidelines should be obtained from the cemetery. If you already own a lot, it is a good idea to contact your cemetery to verify your section, lot number, grave layout, size restrictions, and foundation requirements. This information will be necessary to make your final memorial decision. If a memorial marker is already in place, it can be inscribed at the cemetery.

WHO SHOULD SHOP FOR A MONUMENT?

As in most decisions surrounding a death, it is easier for some families to shop together, and for other families to designate specific members to shop for the monument. Regardless of who does the shopping, keep in mind that this is a major purchase and should receive the same consideration as any other major purchase.

WHAT IS THE COST OF A MARKER?

A carved, inscribed, marker or upright monument could range between $400 and $4,000.

INSCRIPTION

Ellen and I had been talking about having something really unique and specific about us, as individuals, inscribed upon our grave markers, only to discover that most people in today's society want to have something really unique and specific, about them, inscribed upon their grave markers. It is an extremely popular thing to do, and, with the addition of computers and laser etching techniques being added to the world of marker inscription, it is as easy as deciding what you want to say. You can even have an etching of your favorite car, mate, or hobby etched next to your name and dates. Just one more thing to add to that file of things that you want to have done when you are gone!

In geographic areas where the weather turns cold, a stone will not be inscribed until the weather warms because cracking in the stone can occur.

JEWISH TOMBSTONE

Jewish law requires that a tombstone be prepared so that the deceased will not be forgotten and the grave will not be desecrated. It is customary, in some communities, to keep the tombstone veiled, or to delay installation, until the end of the 12-month mourning period. The idea underlying this custom is that the dead will not be forgotten when he or she is being mourned daily. In communities where this custom is observed, there is generally a formal unveiling ceremony when the tombstone is revealed. The ceremony takes approximately five to ten minutes. In some communities the tombstone is unveiled eleven months after the actual funeral burial, and in Israel and many communities abroad, the stone is erected approximately 30 days after death. In the days when there were no tombstones, visitors would each place a stone upon the grave. Over the years, a mound of stones would accumulate memorializing the deceased through the hands of his or her loved ones.

CEMETERY EXPENSES

The charge for a standard two-grave lot is approximately $1,100 but will vary in each part of the country and for each cemetery. The charge for opening and closing of the grave lot is approximately $500. Some cemeteries require installation charges for your marker, and cemeteries usually require that cement foundations be poured before erection of an upright marker. This cost ranges from $100 for removal of grass for a flat marker to a few hundred dollars to dig and pour a foundation for an upright marker. Saturday funerals leaving the cemetery after noon, and weekday funerals leaving the cemetery after 3:30pm, may have an additional expense added to compensate workers for extra hours.

FOUNDATIONS

The foundation is the underlying support for the monument. Some cemeteries prefer to pour the foundation themselves, and others require that you have your monument company pour it. The foundation will prevent the headstone from tipping or sinking as the earth settles. It is usually constructed of cement at a depth that will support the weight of the memorial and withstand the extremes of weather, temperature, and water.

REPARATION OF MONUMENTS

Sometimes, over the years, monuments or old headstones are in need of repairs. The same monument company, that erected the monument, can make the repairs. They can also add, remove, or replace an old foundation in the process.

PURCHASING GRAVE LOTS

Only purchase the number of grave lots that you need. In the old days, people purchased a family lot, but today we are more mobile and families move about. You should purchase at least two grave lots to ensure that you and your companion will be placed together. If you choose to purchase only one lot, your companion may not be able to purchase a lot close to you when it is necessary. If you buy a grave after the fact and try to be buried in the same area, it is called single grave, preferred section, and it may cost you more money.

PLACEMENT INSIDE OR OUTSIDE OF A CEMETERY

In the past, if there was a suicide in a Jewish family, the member had to be buried in the back of the cemetery. It was a very painful reminder for family members. Jewish thinking has now changed and instead of considering it as 'thou shalt not kill' it is considered as an illness and the deceased is treated with the same respect as any other deceased. If there was a suicide in a non-Jewish family, or if the community ostracized a member of the family, the member had to be buried outside the cemetery fence. Many people still remain buried outside of cemetery fences.

GRAVE VAULTS—LINERS AND OUTER BURIAL ENCLOSURES

Although lots may be purchased 10 to 20 years in advance, the cemetery may require that a grave liner, usually concrete, be purchased at the time of use. Members of the family that are handling the prepaid burial arrangements are often surprised by the liner charge. If burial services are purchased in advance, make sure that liner costs are included. Even burial liners come in simple and ornate. If you want something fancier than the simple cement liner, the vault is called an Outer Burial Enclosure. Vaults assist in the digging of graves, as they allow the next grave not to be impeded upon. For burial in some traditional Jewish cemeteries, it may be necessary to have holes drilled in the liner or outer burial enclosure. Check with the individual organization, or synagogue, that owns the cemetery for specific liner requirements.

DOUBLE DEPTH BURIAL

You may prefer to bury in double depths with two people buried in the same vertical space. Double depth graves are usually less expensive than purchasing two separate grave lots and they come in two varieties.

You can bury one on top of the other, like two shoeboxes stacked one on one, or you can purchase a double depth crypt that is more like a cereal box with a shelf or roof separating the two caskets. Some cemeteries allow more than two people to be buried in the same vertical space, but you must check with your cemetery superintendent to find out the specific burial arrangements allowed in your particular cemetery. Grave markers, small slant markers, or monuments may be allowed, but it is a matter of cemetery policy and should be discussed before you purchase your lot.

BURIAL OF CREMAINS

Cemeteries have varying rules and regulations that govern the burial of cremains. Some offer the option of purchasing a small cremation lot. A flat marker of no more than a specific size may be the headstone guideline. Another option might be to purchase a regular size lot, as for a casket, and use it for the burial of cremains. Some cemeteries have no requirement for the number of cremains buried per lot, other cemeteries will allow no more than two. Another choice is to place a cremation urn within the lot of a previously deceased spouse, either set upon the casket, or placed on either side of the headstone. It is best to check with the cemetery in which you wish to have your cremains buried for specific requirements.

RECEIVING VAULT

The final note for cemetery pricing pertains to the holding of a body in the receiving vault. For 3 months or less, the charge for holding services would be approximately $75 depending on the cemetery and the area of the country where the cemetery is located.

WHY WOULD SOMEONE BE PLACED IN A RECEIVING VAULT?

A person would be placed in a receiving vault either because of weather conditions, too cold to work the ground, or by family choice, the body will be moved but the family is undecided where.

WHO ARE CEMETERIANS?

Cemeterians are people who are employed in the cemetery industry—Cemetery Supervisors or Cemetery Sextons.

HOW ARE PRIVATE CEMETERIES GOVERNED?

Private cemeteries have a board of directors and articles of incorporation with specific guidelines that must be followed. Each cemetery operates differently. Some cemeteries have a large employed staff and other cemeteries are run by a small group of volunteers. Speak to the cemetery representative about the cemetery guidelines on cremains, casket burials, plantings, headstones, and any individual traditions your family might observe, prior to choosing a particular cemetery.

GRAVE PLANTINGS

Some cemeteries allow plantings on cemetery lots and others do not. Common practice seems to make ease of grass cutting the deciding factor. Check with cemetery authorities or your family funeral director before planting. If grave markers are allowed, you may choose a design with a plant stand appendage, however, it is difficult to keep plants alive in a cemetery. By their very nature, cemeteries are large expanses of land with minimal shade. Plants tend to dry out quickly unless watered daily by a family member or friend.

TIPS FOR MAKING YOUR FLOWERPOTS AND BOXES STAY PUT

In some cemeteries it seems like you no sooner place the flowerpot or box on the grave and it "walks away." A tip is to place a long L-shaped metal rod in the center of the flowerpot or box before putting the soil and flowers in. Push the rod deep into the ground and anyone wishing to take your flower pot for a walk will have to visibly pull it strenuously from the ground.

ENTOMBMENT

Entombment offers a fixed, final resting-place. When the body is entombed, the casket is placed in a mausoleum—an above ground structure usually made of marble or stone. Mausoleums vary greatly in size and design. Some are large enough for the whole family with separate rooms for each member. Most are found on cemetery grounds, although some are not. Entombment in a large family mausoleum seems to be preferred by people who want the deceased to be remembered as someone who was important in life.

MAUSOLEUM

Mausoleum takes its name from King Mausolos of Halicarnassus, whose wife and queen, Artemisia, had the best artisans of Greece construct a most magnificent tomb upon his death in 356 BCE. This tomb was one of the Seven Wonders of the Ancient World until crusaders seeking stone for a fortress ravaged it. Some of the works of art, which had been contained within this tomb, are now displayed in the British Museum.

Dependent on where you live, and the cemeteries available in your area, there may or may not be a mausoleum option. My father and brother Tom are in a mausoleum, on the top level. Sometimes the top level is the most expensive because it is not as susceptible to vandalism and is closest to the sun; sometimes the eye level position is the most expensive because it is easier to change the flowers. In either case, a mausoleum with chandeliers, flowers, and/or a chapel is an option, if it is available. It allows you to stay out of the ground without being cremated.

VISITING A CEMETERY

There are some concerns about the safety of visiting a cemetery in today's world. Practical safety guidelines should be followed just the same as if you were parking your car in the lot of your favorite shopping mall. Lock your car doors, don't leave your purse or car keys in plain view on the seat, look around and note who is in the area, and do not become so involved in what you are doing that you lose track of your surroundings. Dale J. Fiore of Evergreen Cemetery and Crematory Association says, "If you are visiting a cemetery that has an active supervisor and ground crew, call ahead and tell the supervisor when you will be arriving, stop at the office, beep the horn, and wave. If you are uncomfortable, for any reason, do not get out of your car."

MOVING A BODY TO ANOTHER CEMETERY

Moving a body or buried cremains to another cemetery can be done; however, considerable expense may be involved. Another grave lot must be purchased, the original grave must be opened, a disinterment permit must be obtained, and a funeral director may be required to obtain the transportation permit to provide movement over the road. The longer the deceased has been interred, the greater the risk because, until fairly recent times, liners were not used and the natural return to earth process will have already begun. Disinterment is not allowed for Jewish people except when the following circumstance occurs: a person is buried in the wrong grave, a single person is to be moved into a family plot, or, a person is to be buried in Israel.

BACKFILLING THE DEPRESSED GROUND

A friend of mine asked why Cemeterians don't backfill the depressed ground over newly dug lots when they know that a committal service is going to take place in the immediate vicinity. I asked Dale J. Fiore of Evergreen Cemetery and Crematory Association and this was his reply: "When an area is excavated for burial, the top layers of soil are removed, and the vault is placed. The area is filled with sand to a certain level until the time that it is prepared for grass. It is like removing a piece of a puzzle and then trying to fit it back. The earth has to settle back into place around the new vault. As the area settles it is backfilled slowly over time and when it has reached near ground level the topsoil is prepared with fertilizer and replaced in a slightly crowned manner to allow for additional settling. In the meantime, if a new burial is going to take place in the vicinity, the area will be raked and cleaned as much as possible, but it takes time for nature to settle back to its original condition and it takes time for grass to grow."

WHY IS THE CEMETERY CREW IN VIEW?

Although it is not necessary for the crew to be in view of the family, and in usual circumstances the family should not see the crew, there are certain circumstances when it will occur, such as, on a Saturday if the burial is late in the morning. Cemetery crews finish at 1pm on Saturday. Usually people do not want to pay extra for overtime, so the crew will be ready to move in and finish within their usual work hours. For some families, it is comforting to know that their loved one is not just going to lie in the cemetery waiting for the crew. They find satisfaction in knowing that the body will be buried immediately.

THE RITE OF COMMITTAL (LOWERING THE CASKET OR ENTOMBMENT)

The Order of Christian Funerals, the definitive rite of the Roman Catholic Church since 1989, defines the Rite of Committal as "...the conclusion of the funeral rites. It is the final act of the community of faith in caring for the body of its deceased member. It may be celebrated at the grave, tomb, or crematorium and may be used for burial at sea. Whenever possible, the Rite of Committal is to be celebrated at the site of committal beside the open grave or place of interment, rather than at the cemetery chapel."

6

Mourning

What is life?
It is the flash of a firefly in the night.
It is the breath of a buffalo in the wintertime.
It is the little shadow that runs across the grass
and loses itself in the sunset.
Crowfoot 1821-1890

MOURNING

How much is too much? How little is too little? It seems that we can never mourn the correct amount of time to suit other people. Mourning is one of the most private individual experiences in our lifetime. There is no set time for mourning or for completing the mourning process. Take as long as you need. Get help if you think that it is beyond your ability to cope. And finally, lighten up on yourself and let others think what they will.

THE STAGES OF GRIEF

After someone you love dies, your feelings may seem to have frozen. You will do what you have to do to get through the initial funeral arrangements and legal filings that go along with death, but when you have had time to think about it, you will be amazed that you did. After the initial stage of death, there are stages of grief that can put you on the downward spiral, but as time progresses you will again begin to ascend towards a new life. The first stage of grief towards beginning a new life might be panic at the thought of going through life alone, followed by anger at the loved one who left you behind, but with time you will start to have selected memory of the person who died. You will begin to form new life patterns and eventually you will reach the final stage of grief and you will know that life is okay and you are going to make it on your own. If you need help to cope with these stages of grief, talk with your funeral director. He or she will be able to direct you to someone who can help.

BEREAVEMENT GROUPS

Not everyone needs bereavement counseling. Some people only need someone to talk with who can understand what they are going through. They just need an opportunity to talk about the death of a loved one with someone who has gone through the same experience. Bereavement groups fulfill that need. There is no way to avoid going through the grieving process. You may put the process aside, but it will raise its head somewhere down the road. Putting milk in the cupboard and sugar in the refrigerator are normal grief reactions to death. Your mind is simply on something else. If you didn't know that forgetfulness is a normal part of grieving, you might think that you were losing it. Give yourself time to heal and after a while if you have no good days you may want to join a bereavement group. Look in the newspaper or yellow pages under support groups or contact friends, clergy, or funeral directors. Although you may not believe it, there are a lot of people who can help you.

JEWISH MOURNING—SITTING SHIVA

Jewish mourning can be broken into several periods of decreasing intensity. When a close relative hears of the death of a loved one it is traditional for them to tear their clothing. The tear is made over the heart if a parent has died, over the right side of the chest if it is a close relative. If a person does not tear their clothing, a black ribbon (Kriah) is worn and torn against the grain to symbolize the tearing of cloth. The ribbon is worn on the left chest for a child and to the right side for the spouse and all other close relatives. The significance of the tear is a tearing of the heart. It is torn against the grain so that even if sewn, the tear will always show. The mourner recites the blessing in acceptance of God's taking of the life of a relative. From death to burial, the mourner's responsibility is in caring for the deceased and preparing for the burial. These preparations take first priority. This period lasts a day or two; Judaism requires prompt burial. During the preparation period, the family is left alone and allowed to grieve fully. Condolences are not made during this time. After the burial, a close friend or relative will prepare the first meal for the mourners. It is designed to include foods that symbolize eternal life; round rolls and bagels, oval eggs, and lentils; all symbolic of the cyclical, eternal, continuous nature of life. After serving these ceremonial foods, a regular meal is eaten. The meal is for the family only. After this time of mourning, condolences are permitted.

The next period is commonly referred to as Shiva (seven, because it lasts seven days). The closest relatives, usually all together in the home of the deceased, observe Shiva. Shiva begins on the day of burial and continues until the morning of the seventh day. Mourners sit on low stools or on the floor. They do not wear leather shoes, do not shave or cut their hair, do not wear cosmetics, do not work, and do not do things of comfort or pleasure. These things are signs of wealth. The mourner is not wealthy in their time of loss. Mourners wear the clothes that they tore on learning of the death. The obituary column will tell you if Shiva is strictly private (no visitors) or private (relatives and close friends). You do not speak to the mourner until the mourner speaks to you. You do not have to bring anything; it is just a time to let the mourners know that you care. Prayer services are held where the Shiva is taking place with friends, neighbors, and relatives making up the 10 people necessary for certain prayers to be said.

The subsequent period of mourning is known as shloshim (thirty) because it lasts until the 30th day after burial. During that time, mourners do not attend parties or celebrations, do not shave or cut their hair, and do not listen to music.

The final period of mourning is observed only for a parent. This time lasts for twelve months after the burial. The mourners avoid parties, celebrations, theater, and concerts. For eleven months of that period, starting with the burial, the children of the deceased recite the mourner's prayer every day. After the period of twelve, the family is not permitted to continue formal mourning; however, on the anniversary of the death, family members will observe the anniversary. Mourners light a candle that burns for 24 hours in honor of the decedent and the children recite special prayers. There is a Jewish saying, "You should not mourn too well." After 12 months, the mourning period is considered over.

According to James Shure of Robert Shure Funeral Home, Jewish rules and customs make the lives of family and friends easier to bear. The family lives according to tradition and there are fewer decisions to make at an already difficult time.

MOURNING A TRAUMATIC DEATH

The mourning that comes with traumatic death is different from all other grief because it is sudden, unexpected, and unpredictable. Family members may think that it could have been prevented. Sudden death gives a sense of uneasiness about everyday life. Grief reactions can be extensive and complicated. Family members and friends have to cope with a death for which they had little time to prepare and no time to say their final good-byes. Survivors have strong feelings of anger and guilt and think, "If only this" or "If only that" had occurred or not occurred it would have been different. Sometimes the deceased has been disfigured and survivors anguish over thoughts that the victim might have suffered before he or she died. And, in times of traumatic death, the media is often involved and can make the matter even more difficult for family and friends who are already upset. Many times family members and friends want to "get it over with" and put the death behind them. This is not always best. Sometimes even when trauma strikes, it is necessary to take a step back and evaluate the decisions that you are making and remember the person who died in a personal way that will help alleviate the pain that accompanies the death. Sometimes a funeral, no matter how disfigured the victim, is the time to say good-bye and the time to come to terms with the loss. Funeral Directors can explain to you what to expect and the feelings that you might experience. They can direct you to support groups for survivors of suicides, homicides, accidents, and other traumatic death incidents.

7

The Process of Dying

I have a new appreciation of things I once took for granted:
eating lunch with a friend, scratching my cat Muffet's ears
and listening for his purrs, the company of my wife, reading a
book or magazine in the quiet of my bed lamp at night,
raiding the refrigerator for a glass of orange juice or a slice of toast.
For the first time, I think I actually am savoring life."
Senator Richard L. Neuberger,
When the cancer that later took his life was first diagnosed.
Better Homes and Gardens magazine

THE FOUR STAGES OF TERMINAL ILLNESS

It seems that when a person is diagnosed with a terminal illness there
are four stages through which they must travel, but they may not be in
this particular order.

Denial—The person will usually think that the diagnosis is wrong
and check with a multitude of physicians. Once the diagnosis seems

correct they may try various miracle cures or prayer. Denial basically acts as a buffer that allows a person to accept death slowly.

Anger—The person will ask "Why me?" They may curse God or take out their hostility on everyone around them. They may resent your being healthy when they are not. It is a difficult time for family and friends. It is a difficult time for the person who is dying.

Fear and Depression—The person who is dying may have a fear of death, or a fear of losing his or her family, or losing control, or losing the ability to be useful. The person who is dying may fear the process of dying itself. They may feel guilty because they cannot do the things that they did before they became ill, and they may become depressed over unfulfilled plans for the future and withdraw from their family and friends.

Acceptance—Not all people achieve acceptance, but if a person accepts their fate they become calm and begin their preparations in an orderly manner, discussing their decisions with family and friends.

FAMILY PREPARATION

As the person that you love is dying, you will probably begin working through your sorrow as you prepare for the loss. The first stage may also be denial and the second stage may also be anger, especially if you do not feel that the person you love took care of himself or herself. You may also feel guilty because you are healthy and the person that you love is not. You may be on an emotional roller coaster, always doing your best and hoping that it's enough; trying to be strong, but falling apart inside; and you may need the support of the person that you love, who may no longer be able to give you that support. You may experience panic, or depression, and your own grief may show itself in genuine physical pain. You may need someone to talk to outside of your immediate circle of family or friends. Do not be afraid to seek professional help.

TELLING A CHILD ABOUT DEATH

Telling a child that their father, mother, or grandparent is dying may be a challenge. Children have all kinds of questions. They will be curious. This is a new experience for them. Keep your answers simple and honest. Let children see their relative, but explain that the person may not look or act the same as he or she did the last time the child saw him or her. Your children need to resolve their own grief. Let them see and feel your grief and allow them to learn the grieving process from you. Above all, remember that they are children, and allow them their childhood even though you may be going through a difficult time.

COPING WITH THE DEATH WAIT

Nothing makes the wait for death easy. We don't like to talk about death in our culture and many times the dying person and his or her family ignores the subject entirely. Ignoring the strong emotions that you are feeling won't make them go away. Talk about your feelings and listen to what the person you love has to say. Talk about what you must do to prepare for death. When my sister-in-law Kathy was dying, we were sitting together talking about old times. There was a time when we were very young, I was about 12 and she perhaps 18, and we had dyed her hair dark blue-black while my brother was at work. We didn't know that the dye would make her neck and forehead turn black. We didn't know that you were supposed to put cold cream on your skin before you dyed the hair. We hadn't bothered to read the directions until after her face and neck had turned black. As we recounted the old story, we started to laugh, and our laughter turned to tears, and we cried to think that there would be no new stories to share. Her daughter walked in at that moment and said, "Mom, you're not crying are you? Everything will be okay, just don't cry." Crying is part of grief, and crying is part of life and death. Kathy and I had shared many experiences together in our lives. We knew that there would not be many more experiences to share.

To cry together and hold each other was an extremely comforting way for us to spend the little time that we had left. It was a way for us to uniquely say our personal good-byes in the company of others. It's okay to laugh, and it's okay to cry. It's an extremely emotional time with all emotions close to the surface.

Make sure that you include the dying person in your activities and discussions. Sometimes families treat the dying person as if they are already dead. The person feels lonely and rejected. Many times I have seen people who are visiting a sick person completely leave them out of the conversation and talk around them. Share your stories and talk about what is going on. Keep them active in your family life.

If you are caring for a dying relative, take care of yourself too. Eat well, sleep when you can, and exercise. Physical activity can help offset depression. Perhaps you can schedule a walk with a friend to share feelings and relieve the stress. When my father was dying I used to run with a friend. She felt left out because I never talked about my dad during our runs, but those runs were the most relaxing times of my day. It allowed me time to think and talk about mundane, ordinary events that were of no importance to me. I didn't talk about my dad because it was too hard and I needed time for myself to unwind and enjoy the sunshine. After my run, after my shower, I would call my mom and we would talk about my dad.

Sometimes grief becomes so intense that you will wonder if you need professional help. If you think that you would like professional help ask your clergyman, doctor, or funeral director to suggest a counselor. There are many people who can assist you through the difficulties of coping with dying and death. Check into your employee assistance program. Some companies will pay for employees who need counseling.

HOME • HOSPITAL • HOSPICE

Some people prefer to die at home. It affords them the comfort of familiar surroundings and the ability to maintain some control over their life. If your loved one prefers to die at home, ask your doctor to recommend an in-home medical service to help you. It will allow you the time you need to go out while knowing that the person you love is well taken care of. Do not take the daunting task of home care upon yourself without support.

Hospital care allows the person you love to be well taken care of with the best equipment at hand. The dying person, however, may feel that others determine their time and schedule and they may not like the atmosphere. Some hospitals now have a Hospice wing. Even if you do not move the patient to Hospice, the Hospice staff is available to assist. They share information and written materials on the dying process and, while some of it is difficult to accept it can be comfortable to know what to anticipate. People are also available to help with the emotional trauma of dealing with death. The Hospice section of a hospital, as well as Hospice itself, consists mostly of communal rooms. There are curtains between patients for privacy, when necessary, but many families find comfort in sharing their experience with others who are going through the same helpless watch period. After learning about the dying process you can sometimes gently prepare your loved one and yourself to accept the natural process of dying as it occurs.

Hospice has other alternatives, lending you nurses and equipment while your loved one is at home, and providing them with additional care at a Hospice facility when home care is no longer feasible. Patients can rest and receive excellent care in a Hospice facility, however, Hospice will not supply life support when a person is actively in the process of dying. When my sister-in-law, Kathy, who had cancer, went to Hospice, we knew that no life support would be given. We thought that the statement meant life support equipment, however, it goes beyond that. Kathy was in the final stages of dying when she arrived at Hospice. The nurse said Kathy was much worse than any of us knew. We had not realized that not supplying life support also meant that they would not bring her food: ice cream, tapiocas, etc. Kathy had not been eating for a long time, but the hospital had continued to bring her food. The bringing of the food, and the little that Kathy could eat, seemed to allow her daughter, Kathleen, to think that things were okay. Kathy did not want any food and the nurses at Hospice did not bring it. Kathleen thought that they were starving her mother, but, of course, they were not. They just know the disease and they know what it does to the patient. Most cancer patients cannot eat in the final stages of preparation for death, even though their families think that if the person would just eat something, even a morsel, they would be okay. Hospice is a final step in the process of dying and no life support means no life support. They will provide everything a person needs to be as comfortable as possible at the end of their life. They will try to support the family through the process of dying. They will teach the family about death. They will allow the person that you love to die with dignity in their own time.

For Ellen and her mom, the time hanging out together before her mom died was the best comfort for both of them. It became a cherished opportunity for them to talk, and ease their minds, and to finalize any business that had to be discussed. Both Ellen and her mom obtained a great sense of peace by knowing that the other was there. The Hospice nurses had told Ellen that she should never feel awkward about talking to the doctors or nurses about her mother. To the contrary, they encouraged her to ask questions and to keep the medical staff informed of any changes that she noticed in her mother's condition. As family, you are often the one to fill in the little details that the nurses and doctors may be too busy to attend to.

8

The Living Will

A dying man needs to die, as a sleepy man needs to sleep,
and there comes a time when it is wrong,
as well as useless, to resist.
Stewart Alsop

We decided to begin this section with a definition of terms. In that way you will know the terminology that is used at health care facilities and be able to speak the same language from the beginning.

A LIVING WILL DEALS WITH HEALTH ISSUES.
A GLOSSARY OF TERMS...

Artificial Nutrition & Hydration—delivering food and fluids to the body by means other than by mouth.

Cardiac Arrest—A sudden failure of the heart to function.

Cardiopulmonary Resuscitation (CPR)—Artificial respiration and heart massage to restart the heart and lungs.

Code or Team—The summoning of a special medical team to start CPR and other life support measures when a patient has gone into cardiac or respiratory arrest.

Do Not Resuscitate Order (DNR)—The decision not to initiate CPR, as mutually agreed upon by the patient, family, and physician. (DNR does not mean withholding other types of care or compromising the quality of care.)

Durable Power of Attorney—A legal document in which you appoint another person with the power to make personal decisions should you become unable to make decisions for yourself.

Extubation—Withdrawal of mechanical breathing tubes.

Health Care Agent—A person or persons appointed to communicate your wishes to health-care providers should you become incapacitated.

Informed Consent—Permission given to receive tests, treatments, or procedures after you have been fully informed of their potential benefits and risks.

Intubation—Insertion of a tube, most commonly into the air passages, to provide mechanical breathing for a patient.

Life Support Systems—Any intervention or combination of interventions used to maintain body functions when they are not likely to function on their own.

Living Will—A signed statement made in advance indicating your views and wishes concerning medical care should you become unable to make such decisions for yourself.

Respirator/Ventilator—Types of mechanical devices used to provide assisted breathing for patients with respiratory failure.

THE LIVING WILL

In today's world, health and social service professionals are urging families to consider bio-ethical issues before facing illness. With medical technology now capable of sustaining life almost indefinitely, critical medical treatment choices have become a part of our lives.

To make sure that your choices are known, you can arrange for a "Living Will" detailing your wishes. The most important thing to remember is that your directions should be clear and in writing. A living will is a signed statement made in advance indicating your views and wishes concerning medical care should you become unable to make such decisions for yourself. Two witnesses and a Notary Public must sign it. Ellen's mother had completed her living will several years prior to her illness. The family made extra copies and placed them in their home file. On admittance to the hospital a person is asked if they have a living will. If they do have one, they are asked to bring it to the hospital to be placed in the patient's file. The hospital has forms available for you to complete, if desired, but there is already a lot to think about at the time of illness and admittance. Once the patient leaves the hospital, the copy of the living will is destroyed. A new copy is required for each hospital admittance. When asked why the hospital does not keep that information in the patient's file, the response was that a living will could be changed, and updated, at any time. The hospital wants to be assured that, with each hospital admittance, they have the most current copy. Keeping multiple copies is a great idea for everyone involved.

As Ellen's mother's condition changed, her doctor reviewed the directives as laid out in the living will before deciding what actions the hospital staff would take, or not take, in relation to her condition. Ellen, as her mother's Health Care Agent, felt that she clearly understood the potential consequences of the directives as laid out in the living will.

The key to informed choice is full and open communication among all concerned: patient, family members, physicians, and others. Ask the physician questions that will help you to understand the medical problems and treatment options that are available to you. Do not be afraid to express fears and concerns. The more open you are with the physician and health care providers, the better they are able to help you and realize the sensitivity of your wishes.

Many questions do not have easy answers. They depend on what you and your family want, your values, your religious beliefs, and the quality of life that you want to maintain for the individual.

THINGS THAT YOU SHOULD KNOW ABOUT A LIVING WILL

A living will would not take precedence in an emergency situation. If you call an ambulance or a paramedic, the person in charge will automatically initiate emergency procedures that may or may not include extraordinary means of keeping a person alive.

SHOULD A LIVING WILL EVER BE CHANGED?

Yes, like all things that change in life, a living will should be updated as the need arises.

MAKING THE RIGHT DECISIONS FOR YOU AND YOUR FAMILY

Questions that you may wish to consider…

What rights and responsibilities do members of my family or I have in making choices about treatment?

Do I have enough information to make these choices?

If I am unable to make decisions for myself, who would decide for me: my family, physician, clergy, attorney, or close friend?

What if my heart stops? Should resuscitation procedures be done? Would the answer be different if a chronic, debilitating or terminal illness were involved?

Will certain choices create an undue financial burden on my family, or me, especially if the outcome is certain death?

If the illness were terminal, at what point would I say, "Enough is enough. Please just keep me comfortable."

Should life-prolonging treatments continue?

Have my family members and I made our wishes known? Have we discussed all of the important questions with our physician and family members?

ADVANCE DIRECTIVE

An advance directive is any signed and witnessed statement (such as a Living Will, Appointment of Health Care Agent, or Durable Power of Attorney for a Health Care Agent) that sets forth your wishes should you be unable to make a decision yourself.

DURABLE POWER OF ATTORNEY FOR HEALTH CARE AGENT

A durable power of attorney for health care agent is a legal document in which you appoint another person with the power to make personal decisions should you become unable to make decisions for yourself.

The hospital, or health care facility, should have a new copy on file each time that the patient is admitted. It can also be updated at any time. Be sure that the facility has the latest copy. This allows the health care providers to know who should be consulted if you become totally incapacitated and can no longer make your own decisions on critical issues. The health care agent appointed by you will make those decisions for you. As long as you are able, you will be kept completely informed and you will make the decisions.

A sample form is attached which requires a witness and a notarized signature page. Your attorney, and usually your health care providers, will also have the forms available. It is easier to complete these forms and make multiple copies before you need them rather than when you are in a crisis situation. You can give them to the hospital as needed.

STATUTORY SHORT FORM DURABLE POWER OF ATTORNEY

In addition to an Appointment of Health Care Agent, this form is broader appointing a Power of Attorney to act on your behalf should you become incapacitated to act on your own in legal matters. A form that is specific to your state can be obtained from your attorney. This form may specify, by you, that a designated person can act on your behalf in real estate transactions; chattel and goods transactions; bond, share, and commodity transactions; banking transactions; business operating transactions; insurance transactions; estate transactions; claims and litigation; personal relationships and affairs; benefits from military service; records, reports, and statements; health care decisions; and all other matters.

This form is also to be witnessed and notarized. Multiple people can be identified on individual forms for separate transactions. Multiple copies can be made and maintained in your files. These forms can be updated, as you wish, as circumstances change.

LIVING WILL—SAMPLE

Directive made this_____day of_____(month, year).

I_____, having the capacity to make health care decisions willfully and voluntarily make known my desire that my dying shall not be artificially prolonged under the circumstances set forth below, and do hereby declare that:

(a) If at any time I should be diagnosed in writing to be in a terminal condition by the attending physician, or in a permanent unconscious condition by two physicians, and where the application of life sustaining treatment would serve only to artificially prolong the process of my dying, I direct that such treatment be withheld or withdrawn, and that I be permitted to die naturally.

I understand by using this form that a terminal condition means an incurable and irreversible condition caused by injury, disease, or illness, that would within reasonable medical judgment cause death within a reasonable period of time in accordance with accepted medical standards, and where the application of life sustaining treatment would serve only to prolong the process of dying.

I further understand in using this form that a permanent unconscious condition means an incurable and irreversible condition in which I am medically assessed within reasonable medical judgment as having no reasonable probability of recovery from an irreversible coma or a persistent vegetative state.

(b) In the absence of my ability to give directions regarding the use of such life sustaining treatment, it is my intention that this directive shall be honored by my family and physician(s) as the final expression of my legal right to refuse medical or surgical treatment and I accept the consequences of such refusal. If another person is appointed to make these decisions for me, whether through a durable power of attorney or otherwise, I request that the person be guided by this directive and any other clear expressions of my desires.

(c) If I am diagnosed to be in a terminal condition or in a permanent unconscious condition (check one):

I DO want to have artificially provided nutrition and hydration.
I DO NOT want to have artificially provided nutrition and hydration.

(d) If I have been diagnosed as pregnant and my physician knows that diagnosis, this directive shall have no force or effect during the course of my pregnancy.

(e) I understand the full import of this directive and I am emotionally and mentally capable to make the health care decisions contained in this directive.

(f) I understand that before I sign this directive, I can add to or delete from or otherwise change the wording of this directive and that I may add to or delete from this directive at any time and that any changes shall be consistent with_____
state law or federal constitutional law to be legally valid.

(g) It is my wish that every part of this directive be fully implemented. If for any reason any part is held invalid it is my wish that the remainder of my directive be implemented.

(h) Other specific requests: _____

_____

_____

_____

_____

Signature: _____

The declarer has been personally known to me, and I believe him or her to be capable of making health care decisions.

Witness: _____ Witness: _____
Address: _____ Address: _____

Phone: _____Phone: _____

NOTARIZATION:

On this_____day of_____, 20_____ , before me per-
sonally appeared known to be the individual described in and who executed the foregoing Living Will and acknowledged that he/she signed
said document as his/her free and voluntary act and deed for the uses
and purposes therein mentioned.

IN WITNESS WHEREOF, I have hereunto set my hand and official
seal this_____day of_____, 20_____.

Notary Public in and for the state of _____

This is just a sample.

We recommend that you speak to your physician about the specific
form needed in your particular area or State.

DURABLE POWER OF ATTORNEY FOR HEALTH CARE—SAMPLE

BY THIS DOCUMENT I intend to create a Durable Power of Attorney for Health Care under chapter_____revised code of _____(state).

APPOINTMENT: I, _____,
do hereby appoint (name) _____,
(address)_____

_____, as my attorney-in-fact for health care decisions, granting him/her the authority to consent or refuse consent to any care, treatment, or procedure to treat or maintain my physical or mental condition. This power of attorney shall become effective upon my mental incompetence or loss of decision-making capacity. If protective procedures are commenced, I nominate my attorney-in-fact as the guardian of my person.

DIRECTIONS: In exercising this authority, my attorney-in-fact shall make decisions consistent with my desires concerning use of life-sustaining procedures as stated in my Health Care Directive (Living Will) or otherwise communicated or expressed.

AUTHORITY: In the event of my loss of decision-making capacity, my attorney-in-fact shall have all the powers, discretions, and rights that I would have, if competent or retaining decision-making capacity, to consent to my medical surgical or hospital care, to consent to the provision, withholding or withdrawal of life-sustaining procedures, to consent to my admission to or transfer from a health care facility, and to decide the disposition of my remains.

DOCUMENTS: My attorney-in-fact shall have the authority to execute any documents giving informed consent, refusing or terminating treatment, or waivers or releases of liability required by a health care provider.

INDEMNITY: My attorney-in-fact shall have no personal liability for my expenses incurred or acts performed while acting in good faith under the terms of this document. I hold harmless and indemnify the attorney-in-fact from all expenses incurred on my behalf.

DURATION: This power of attorney for health care will continue in force from the date executed until revoked by my oral or written notice to my attorney-in-fact or to my physician or other health care provider.

ALTERNATIVES: If the person named above as my attorney-in-fact is not that person's appointment as my attorney-in-fact, then I appoint the following persons to serve as my alternate attorney-in-fact to make health care decisions for me. Such persons are to serve in the order listed:

First alternate _____

                insert name and address

Second alternate _____

                insert name and address

SIGNATURE:

I sign my name to this Durable Power of Attorney for Health Care on this____ day of_____, 20___, at (city) ____ (state) _____.

Signature: _____

NOTARIZATION:

On this_____day of_____, 20____, before me personally appeared known to be the individual described in and who executed the foregoing Durable Power of Attorney for Health Care and acknowledged that he/she signed said document as his/her free and voluntary act and deed for the uses and purposes therein mentioned.

IN WITNESS WHEREOF, I have hereunto set my hand and official seal this _____day of _____, 20_____.

Notary Public in and for the state of _____

ACCEPTANCE OF APPOINTMENT:

I agree to serve as attorney-in-fact for health care decisions for _____ and agree to act in a manner consistent with his/her Health Care Directive (Living Will) or as otherwise communicated or expressed. I understand that this document gives me authority for health care decisions only if the declarant becomes incompetent or loses decision-making capacity, and that this authority may be revoked at any time.

signature of attorney-in-fact and date: _____

signature of first alternate and date: _____

signature of second alternate and date: _____

This is just a sample.

We recommend that you speak to your attorney about the specific form needed in your particular area or State.

9

Estate Planning

Anybody has a right to evade taxes if he can get away with it.
No citizen has a moral obligation to assist in maintaining the
government.
J. Pierpont Morgan

Ellen, Bob Bailey, and I are not experts in the field of estate planning or will preparation, nor do we claim to be. The information gathered here is general information that will give you food for thought, but, when it is time for you to prepare your future plans, take the time to do so wisely and secure expert assistance. Under no circumstances will the publisher or the authors be responsible for any incorrect or incomplete information provided here, or for any lost profits or other consequential damages resulting therefrom.

YOUR ESTATE PLAN

During your lifetime you may receive property from various members of your family, and you may pass that property on to your children or grandchildren. Approximately seven out of eight people die without a will allowing $100 million to pass through probate courts each week. Many people work their whole lifetime to provide for their family. It is important to see that your estate is passed on as you wish.

WHAT ARE THE OBJECTIVES OF AN ESTATE PLAN?

- To reduce state and federal estate taxes
- To reduce lawyer's fees, probate costs, and other fees
- To reduce income and gift taxes
- To treat all children fairly, but not necessarily equally
- To keep a business in the family
- To help one or more children start a business
- To reward certain children for specific contributions they have made to their parents or to the estate
- To inform heirs what to expect so they can plan accordingly
- To clearly define your intentions
- To support the charitable causes that you desire

It is okay if some of your objectives conflict. They can be worked out. The most important thing is to plan for the efficient passage of your estate to the next generation.

GENERAL GUIDELINES

- Consider alternate plans until you find the one that suits you and your family best.
- Financial security for your spouse should be high on the priority list. A spouse should have a comfortable home and enough income to take care of themselves.
- Discuss various proposals if children are going to be taking over a business. These discussions should be taken on by the current

owners of the business and should contribute to the general interest and welfare of the entire family.

WHY ARE LIQUID RESERVES NECESSARY?

Liquid reserves are necessary to settle estate debts. Bills, outstanding debts, and taxes must be paid first and these expenses require money. Unless cash is available through insurance or some other source, property may have to be sold at a possible loss.

DOES AN ESTATE PLAN REQUIRE BUSINESS ADVICE FROM A LAWYER AND OTHER PROFESSIONALS?

After you have considered the alternatives a lawyer may be a part of your plan. Working out the details, applying the laws, and drafting and drawing up the legal documents are within their expertise. Other business advice that you may wish to take advantage of includes: an accountant or financial advisor to provide estate analysis, investment advice, information on your business, and tax counseling; trust officers to provide financial advice, trust information, and the suggestions of other competent estate planning professionals who can help including life insurance agents who can analyze the estate owner's insurance policies and plans and agents who are Chartered Life Underwriters (C.L.U.) who are specially trained in estate planning.

Once you have begun an estate plan, take the necessary action steps to achieve the result. Keep your plan current by reviewing and revising it at regular intervals. As conditions, family composition, laws, or financial situations change—revise the plan.

WHAT CAN YOU EXPECT OF A GOOD PLAN?

A good plan can provide financial security for you and your family now and in the future and it may save estate taxes and estate-settlement costs. It can protect your family from quarrels and can avoid the forced sale of property.

WHAT IS A WILL?

A will is a written document that describes how its maker wants property distributed after his or her death. It is the blueprint that guides the court in the distribution of an estate. By making a will a person can decide who shall receive property, how much each shall receive, when they shall receive it, and to some degree what they can do with it. A person who makes a will is called a testator. A person who dies is called a decedent. When a person dies leaving a will, he is said to have died testate. A person who dies without leaving a will dies intestate. A will has no effect during the testator's lifetime. Only upon death does a will disposing of the testator's property become effective to carry out the plans and wishes detailed in the will.

WHO CAN MAKE A WILL?

Any person 18 years or older who is of sound mind and free of any improper or undue influence by another person when the will is made.

WHEN SHOULD A WILL BE MADE?

A will should be made while the maker is in good health and free from emotional stress. A will that is planned quickly and drafted under pressure seldom does credit to the maker or the drafter. The "deathbed" will is the worst since it is usually the subject of long, expensive litigation.

CAN A PERSON WRITE HIS OR HER OWN WILL?

Yes, but it must be completely handwritten entirely in the handwriting of the person making the will. This type of will is called a holographic will. It must be dated and signed. Your handwriting must be legible, and the will must explain clearly what you are leaving and to whom. Your family, friends, and a probate judge must be able to understand your exact wishes in order for the will to be valid. A handwritten will does not have to be notarized or witnessed, but having the will signed by witnesses is a good idea, and, since probate laws are very specific, you may want a lawyer to review the will to be sure that everything is done correctly. A self-made will can be denied probate because of errors, just as any other will can be denied probate. Handwritten wills are recognized in about 25 states and are not highly recommended.

CAN A PERSON USE A FORM WILL?

Some states allow you to use a fill-in-the-blank form will. The form will is designed for single, married, and divorced people with modest estates. It helps you leave your estate to your children or spouse, and lets you give money to one person or charity. With the form you also can name a guardian and executor. Fill-in-the-blank form wills can usually be found in office supply stores.

WHAT MAKES A WILL LEGAL?

You must be of "sound mind." The will must be typewritten or printed on a computer printer except as above (holographic). You must be at least 18 years old in all states except Wyoming where you must be at least 19 years old. The will must have at least one substantive piece of property to leave to someone. You must appoint at least one executor. You must date the will. You must sign the will in front of two witnesses (3 in Vermont). Witnesses must be of sound mind, over 18 years old, and people who won't inherit under the will.

DO WITNESSES HAVE TO KNOW WHAT THE WILL STATES?

No, they must watch you sign and be told that it is your will that they are signing. They do not have to read it or know what it contains.

MUST A WILL BE WITNESSED

A holographic will (one that you have written yourself) does not have to be signed by witnesses. Other wills must be signed by at least two persons who witnessed the signing of the will. In all cases, the testator must sign the will.

A WILL PREPARED BY AN ATTORNEY

An attorney can help you understand the many ways that you can leave your property to your heirs. They can also help you develop a complete estate plan and explain the tax consequences. At least two people who will not inherit from you must see you sign a typed or printed will. These witnesses must also sign your will.

DOES A PARENT HAVE TO LEAVE ANYTHING TO CHILDREN ?

No. Children have no vested interest in their parents' property. Attorneys will name all children to show that the testator did not forget any of them. Otherwise, a child could contest a will claiming his parent unintentionally omitted him or her. If a testator fails to provide in his will for any child, born or adopted after the execution of his will, the omitted child may claim under certain conditions, a share in the estate equal in value to that which he would have received if the testator had died intestate.

DOES DIVORCE, ANNULMENT, OR SEPARATION EFFECT A WILL?

Divorce or annulment revokes the disposition of property made by the will to the former spouse. A separation decree that does not terminate the status of husband and wife is not considered a divorce. Any disposition made in a will to a spouse who is legally separated is still effective.

WHY DO YOU NEED A WILL?

A will is a critical tool in estate planning. If you die without a will the property is distributed in the way that state law dictates. If you have a will, your property is distributed according to your wishes. If you make the estate decisions now, your descendants will face fewer problems at the time of your death. In a will you may direct how you want your property divided after your death, you may name the person you want to handle your estate, you can decrease the expenses of administering your estate, you can save taxes (especially if you have a relatively large estate), you can establish a trust for the support and education of your minor children without court proceedings, and you may appoint a guardian for your minor children.

PREPARING A WILL

The first step to preparing a will is to inventory the property that you own. List what you own, how it is owned, and its estimated value. Check jointly owned properties as it may transfer according to the deed and cannot be willed. If property is held in a joint tenancy with right of survivorship, the person surviving receives the property.

After preparing your list of properties, decide whom you want to receive your property and give full names and addresses. List the debt you owe and the debts owed you. Include how much is owed, who is owed, and how payments are being made.

In your will, you may appoint an executor of your estate and give that person the authority to execute the affairs of the estate. The duties include: retaining a lawyer, setting up a record of accounts for the estate, collecting and paying bills for the estate, handling all the paperwork for the estate, helping with distribution of property, and filing tax forms and paying taxes owed.

Be specific in your will about gifts for specific people; jewelry for sentimental reasons, furniture to designated people, etc. Specify the distribution of your residual estate, the part of your estate left after specific gifts have been given.

If you are married, you may want a simultaneous death clause assuming which spouse dies first if deaths are determined to be simultaneous. This only comes into play when property distribution would be affected by death sequence.

Parents may select guardians for minor children. All people selected should know of your choice before it is specified and they should agree to it.

Any work that you do before you hire an attorney saves you money if the attorney charges an hourly rate. Taking an inventory of property, getting records together, and knowing what you want to include in your will reduces the time that your attorney has to spend on your plan. Use legal advice to ensure that your plans and documents are legally correct and that you have considered all the alternatives. A sample form follows as a tool.

A letter of last instruction should be made available to your executor. The letter should include funeral arrangements; notification list; reasons for unusual statements in the will; names and addresses of guardians, executor, trustee, and lawyer; and any other records and information that would help in the smooth settlement of your estate.

Having a will is important if you want your property distributed, as you would like. Having a will does not reduce estate taxes.

WHO SHOULD KNOW ABOUT THE WILL?

No one needs to know what your will says except your attorney, but your executor/executrix and relatives should know that you have a will and they should know where you keep it. The person chosen, as executor/executrix should be made aware that you have chosen them to fulfill that responsibility. It is important that someone knows where the original will is stored, and, if you add a codicil (supplement, amendment, or addition) to your will, it should be stored in the same place. If your original will is stored in your safe deposit box, be sure that someone knows the location of the key and the location of the safe deposit box. If this information is kept with your attorney, you should advise your executor/executrix or family member of whom your attorney is. If you don't want to have your executor/executrix listed on your safe deposit box, consider keeping your will in another place where it can be collected at death.

The bank never has an additional key to a safe deposit box. There are initially up to three keys. The owner of the box holds two—the bank holds one. If there are two names on the safe deposit box each person can hold a key, if the owner wishes. It takes two keys—one belonging to the owner of the box and one held by the bank to be inserted simultaneously for the safe deposit box to be opened. If you are listed on the safe deposit box, but do not have a key, there is a charge of $100 for the bank to have the lock drilled off the box. The Probate Court will not legally appoint a person as executor/executrix of an estate without the original will. In Connecticut the bank, on notice of death, does not automatically seal a safe deposit box. Check the regulations in your state.

We cannot state emphatically enough the importance of the original will. A copy of the will is not legal. It is not like other documents where a copy is good enough. It has to be the original.

DOES A WILL COVER EVERYTHING YOU OWN?

No. Some property is not covered by a will. Money from your life insurance policy goes to the people you name as beneficiaries on the policy no matter who is listed as an heir in the will. Money from your retirement plan goes to the person you name in the plan. If you own real estate, cars, bank accounts, and other property with another person or persons as joint tenants, your co-owners will inherit your share. Any property that you place in a living trust during your lifetime goes to the trust's beneficiary. A living trust is a way of managing your funds and investments during your lifetime and transferring them to a beneficiary after your death. IRA funds will go to the beneficiaries named or according to your will specifications, or, if no one has been named, as state law designates.

PROPERTY OWNERSHIP

How you own your property is important because it determines how assets can be transferred. For joint tenancies, each spouse will be deemed to hold one-half the value of the property, regardless of who furnished the money to purchase it. When property goes directly to a survivor, all other transfer options that could be used to reduce taxes for the family are lost. Property owned in a joint tenancy with right of survivorship means that each owner owns "part of all" of the property and when one joint owner dies, the property goes to the survivor. A tenancy by the entirety is a joint tenancy between a husband and wife. The usual alternative method of jointly owning property is as tenant in common. Each owner in a tenancy in common owns "all of a part" and only that part is considered in the person's estate.

The importance of holding property in a joint tenancy or in a tenancy in common depends on the size of the estate, the balance of the estate between a husband and wife, and the wishes of the couple transferring the property.

The major advantage of owning property jointly with right of survivorship is that the property goes directly to the survivor and does not pass through probate proceedings. The major disadvantages of holding property in joint tenancy or tenancy by entirety are the loss of control of the property because it cannot be willed by either party and the estate tax problems that occur when all the property goes to the survivor. Joint tenancy ownership causes difficulties in using trusts, and creditors of one party may be able to reach the property in meeting claims. Problems are amplified if divorce occurs.

An advantage of owning property as tenants in common is that each owner can transfer the part owned through a will. A disadvantage is that the transfer is subject to probate proceedings and there may be additional costs.

FINANCIAL WILL—QUESTIONNAIRE—SAMPLE WILL, ADVANCE DIRECTIVE, POWER OF ATTORNEY

Date: _____

Client: _____Spouse: _____

Soc. Sec. No. _____Soc. Sec. No. _____

Address: _____

Family Members

(include children, grandchildren, and all heirs at law whether or not proposed beneficiaries)

name	relationship	date of birth	current address

Disposition plan: _____

Personal effects   Yes   No

To whom? (name and address)

_____

_____

_____

Specific bequests (if any): _____

Item or Amount   To whom (name and address)

_____

_____

_____

_____

Residuary (entitled to the residue of an estate) **Beneficiaries:**

_____

Primary (name and address)   Amount (percent or fraction)

_____

_____

_____

Alternate (name and address):

_____

_____

_____

Trust for Children: Yes   No
If "Yes" age or ages of distributions
% or fraction   at age

% or fraction   at age

% or fraction   at age

*Fiduciaries (name and address)

Executor _____

Alternate_____

Trustee _____

Alternate_____

Guardian _____

Alternate_____

*   If firm member is named as Executor or Alternate complete section headed To be completed if any firm member is named as fiduciary—of this form

Complete estimate of assets on Schedule A to determine if tax planning is needed. Obtain or make a list of life insurance coverage, company names, policy numbers and amounts.

Power of Attorney   Yes   No

Attorney in Fact:

Name: _____Address: _____
Attorney in Fact:
Name: _____Address: _____
To act: severally   joint

Advance Directive   Yes   No

Life Support   Yes   No

Healthcare Agent:

Name: _____Address: _____
Alternate:
Name: _____Address: _____

Conservator:

Name: _____Address: _____

Alternate:

Name: _____Address: _____

Anatomical Gift   Yes   No

Specify

_____

_____

_____

_____

_____

_____

TO BE COMPLETED IF ANY FIRM MEMBER IS NAMED AS FIDUCIARY—

Funeral Instructions:

Funeral home to be used for arrangements:

_____

_____

Pre-need funeral contract purchased?   Yes   No

Cremation: Yes   No

Cemetery for interment:

_____

_____

_____

Lot already purchased: Yes   No

Lot Number: _____   Section: _____

Special Instructions:

_____

_____

_____

_____

_____

SCHEDULE A—INVENTORY AND CLASSIFICATION OF ASSETS

How are they owned? Husband, joint, wife

Personal effects & furnishings:

_____

_____

_____

_____

Automobiles:

_____

_____

_____

Listed Securities:

_____

_____

_____

Savings Accounts:

_____

_____

_____

Checking Accounts:

_____

_____

_____

Residences:

_____

_____

_____

Life Insurance Policies:

_____

_____

_____

This questionnaire is to be used as a worksheet.

You should visit an attorney to discuss the writing of your actual will.

10

Cultural Practices

CULTURE AND BURIAL PRACTICES

Surprisingly, we found many similar practices among the traditions of various people that we researched. All practices were based on respect for the deceased and support of the family.

Burials are still the most common. The body is bathed and dressed or wrapped in traditional clothes or materials. A wake or visitation is common in all but Jewish tradition.

We found that it was important in many traditions that someone stay with the deceased until the time of burial, and many cultures watch as the casket is lowered into the earth and the first handful or shovel full of soil is tossed upon it. In the U.S., many of us have given up that tradition, but the sound of the earth hitting the casket psychologically confirms that the person is indeed gone.

When offering respect, if you know that the traditions of the deceased's family are different from your own, you should stand aside for a few minutes and watch how others interact and then emulate their behavior. As a friend of the family, they will understand that your condolences are given with the utmost respect.

We found that there are unique differences in the traditions of the Navajo culture with regard to death. The deceased are not spoken of in name. The burial is swift, within the day, if possible, and it is very private. The body is bathed, dressed, and buried with great care. Those who attended to the deceased call for a special traditional ceremony and cleansing of themselves. The Navajo traditions are steeped in beliefs of their gods, witches, and traditional ceremonies.

In respect of cultural traditions and deep seated beliefs, sensitivity in addressing people of all cultures during a time of death, whether family or friends, will indicate your own respect for others.

DEATH IN INDIA—HINDU RITES

Death in India, like most things in India, is taken for granted. You are put here, you live out your life, and destiny decides your fate. Upon the death of the oldest member of the family, all family members will gather from near and far, whether the deceased is a man or a woman. I will share with you the Hindu traditions of Kerala, India, for those are the ones that my friend, Murale Gopinathan, and his mother, Ponnamma, have shared with me. Hinduism throughout India is practiced somewhat differently in different areas so there may be some variance.

Upon the death of any family member, the local people will go and cut a mango tree. While the people of the community lay the mango limbs, the Karman (person who performs the ceremony) will wash the deceased and wrap him in white cloth for cremation. Cremation is usually performed within 24 hours because it is hot in Kerala. Once the mango limbs have been properly laid the body will be placed upon the limbs and more limbs will be set on top. The local people will make a little fire out of the husk of the rice patty and the outer shell of a coconut that will be placed in the center of the body and mango tree limbs. The outside of the coconut shell burns very hot and this combination of husks of the rice patty and outer shell of the coconut will burn like a pilot light. The limbs of the mango tree will be used to fuel a huge fire. When the body has been reduced to bone fragments, one bone will be taken from the head, one from the chest, and one from the leg. These bones will be placed in a special place within the garden for one year. Each evening the oil light will be lit by the wife, or special family member, and prayers will be said. Upon the death of a man, his wife will remove the bindi* from her forehead. This is the only time that she has been without the bindi and she will feel very vulnerable without it. Fifteen days after cremation, the oldest son will conduct the first ceremony. There will be fasting until afternoon when the ceremony begins, and the ceremonies will last for three days. All family members and friends will gather. There will be hundreds, and sometimes thousands, of people in attendance. Food will be provided every day for all three days. On the third day the biggest ceremony will be held and everyone will come. At the end of many rituals performed by the eldest son along with a Brahmin priest, the cremated remains will be carried to the river and set upon the water. A big party will then be held to celebrate the person's return from whence he came.

After one year, the oil will no longer be lit, the three bones from the body of the deceased will be set upon the water, and the bindi will be restored to the forehead of the deceased's wife. The official time of mourning will be complete.

In Chennai, India, a woman will shave her head when her husband dies and her head will remain shaved for the rest of her life. This will be the first time that her hair will have been cut.

* The bindi is most commonly known as a red dot on the forehead of an Indian woman, but it is not necessarily so. In India some women change the bindi every time that they change their clothes. Some bindis are sold on a sheet. The bindi peels off and is placed on the forehead.

Bindis come in many sizes and shapes. The bindi is as individual as the woman herself. Some are a black line drawn straight down, approximately 1/2 inch in size; others are circles drawn in red from 1/16 to 1/2 inch round; and sometimes sandalwood paste is put on the forehead to signify the offering of pooja to the gods. I have heard many stories of the bindi. It has been worn for centuries in India to signify the beauty of the woman who wears it. One story is that a warrior, before he went off to battle, pricked his thumb and placed a drop of blood on the forehead of his woman to signify his love of the woman and his safe return. It is also believed to signify the third eye.

KOREAN TRADITION

Koreans frame the tombs of their parents with pine trees that represent the number of children born to them. Sometimes a tablet is placed to the side of the tomb and the names of all the children and grandchildren, and the parents and grandparents of both families are carved in a single column of Chinese characters or in a series of grouped characters. Following the Buddhist tradition, a series of Buddhist prostrations before the grave will be performed ending with the person's forehead touching the earth—filial reverence.

RASTAFARIAN TRADITION

The Rastafari believed that they would never die as long as they remained true and faithful to Selassie. If a Rasta died, it was believed that he had departed from the chosen path and violated some divine precept. Rasta brethren, therefore, did not attend funerals. The general attitude of death was fear of contamination, so Rastafarians totally separated themselves from it. However, there are two kinds of brethren: one that believe that man is put here to live forever, and the other that man is put here but for a time.

MADAGASCAN DEATH DANCE

Madagasy remove the remains of their ancestors from their tombs, dance with the corpses, rewrap them carefully, and place them back into the tombs. "Famadihana—turning of bones" continues a strong tradition of ancestor worship. Relatives and friends toast the occasion with beer and soda while songs blast from amplifiers at all-night dance parties.

11

Death Alternatives

When I told my son Chris that I was writing this book, he said that, if I was talking about the choices that lie beyond, I should not stop with current choices, but should explore beyond the usual. So, in an attempt to expand our horizons, I have looked into death alternatives and found the following:

CREMATION SOCIETIES

The Cremation Society movement started on the West Coast several decades ago as an alternative for consumers interested in simple cremation. Nearly all cremation societies are membership organizations that charge a small non-refundable fee. One of the appeals of cremation societies is their convenience. Complete cremation arrangements can be made by mail, over the telephone, or at your home. Cremation societies specialize in cremations. They do not perform traditional funeral services. To join a cremation society you must fill out a basic information form and pay the membership fee. If you are enrolled in a society, you will be given a membership card. Fees for direct cremation to members nationwide range between $450-$1050. If you are interested in joining a cremation society you can find more information on the Internet at www.cremation.org (The Internet Cremation Society).

CREMAINS IN SPACE

If you are interested in having your cremains released into space, you can contact Celestials, a Houston, Texas, based company that is pioneering the Ashes to Stardust Program. The first launch took off in March of 1997 with the ashes of Gene Roddenberry, creator of Star Trek, and 24 other people aboard. The capsule will orbit the earth as briefly as 18 months or as long as 10 years before it burns up in the atmosphere creating the effect of a shooting star.

MUMMIFICATION

I had thought that mummification went out with the Egyptians, but upon searching the Internet, I have found that is has not. The written word of Summum says, "With today's modern chemistry, mummification treats the body so well that the genetic message within each of the cells is preserved to a very high degree. It is so perfect that the genetics can remain intact for an indefinite amount of time. Mummification has much to offer. Not only does it provide an alternative to current burial methods that accomplish little more than sanitary disposal of the deceased; it provides a burial of distinction and a heightening of our cultural standards. It allows us to experience facets of life unknown to most people. Mummification is such a profound and exact science, its re-emergence may very well change the course of humankind." If you are interested in mummification as a death alternative, check out the Web: Mummification—A Philosophical Examination.

CRYONICS

Cryonics is the technology of freezing a person after death, in the hope that medical science will be able to revive that person, in the future, when life extension and anti-aging have become a reality. Using the example of hypothermia where patients underwent cardiac arrest and there was no brain activity, after the blood was warmed and primed the cells began functioning again and life resumed. The cost of cryonic suspension ranges from $50,000 to $120,000, but even a low or middle income person can afford it by taking out an insurance policy and naming the Cryonics Extension Foundation as the beneficiary. If you are interested in more information about cryonics, notify Alcor Foundation, 7895 E. Acoma Dr., #110, Scottsdale AZ 85260-6916, or call them at 800-367-2228, or look on the Internet at www.alcor.org.

TAXIDERMY

I do not think that taxidermy is actually a choice at this time, but Chris thought that he might like to be stuffed and put in my office at some future date, so I pursued the issue. I have read Grant's Sidewalk Taxidermy and the Low Tech Guide to Preserving Your Friends and Foes on the Internet. It was interesting reading and gave me a lot of insight into taxidermy, but I don't think that it's an option that anyone in their right mind would choose any time soon. The article came with notes stating that, "It is illegal to kill people for taxidermy purposes, and, some North American municipalities require permits to preserve human beings." So, Grant concluded that perhaps taxidermy was an option that existed in the past.

This ends my brief list of death alternatives. The choices that lie beyond seem to be much vaster than we had originally envisioned. We do not sanction, nor advise you to use, any of the methods listed above. We share this information merely to inform.

12

Conclusion

During the writing of this book we spoke with many people. Although each family and each death is different and unique we found that there are basic concepts that people feel strongly about—being treated with respect even after death, and having their body treated in a dignified manner. We found that all of the professionals that we spoke with treat death as a very special life experience. They were deeply concerned about the living as well as the dead and they took their professions very seriously. We hope that this book will help you as much as it has helped us and we hope that you will learn from it and be able to make the difficult choices that lie beyond in an educated manner.

Marble crypts and leaded stained glass combine to form a lasting tribute of inspiration Greenwood Mausoleum, Fort Worth, Texas, USA

As Ellen was rambling through Ireland, she came upon this fantastic cemetery.

Within the beauty of Roussillon, in the Vaucluse hills of Provence, France, the village houses are tinted intensely with colors ranging from golden yellow to the brightest of reds. It was in this village that we came upon a small cemetery (shown on next page). Our driver/guide advised me not to enter. "It is not good," he told me, but I could not be deterred. The cemetery is most beautiful and speaks well for the people who live in the village. There are many flowers, and decorations, and the graves are well maintained.

I AM WRITING THIS AT THE CAPE,
IN FRONT OF THE SEA, WHERE THREE WATERS
MEET AND FURNISH A SIGHT UNEQUALLED
IN THE WORLD. FOR THIS IS NO PORT OF
CALL FOR VESSELS. LIKE THE GODDESS,
THE WATERS AROUND ARE VIRGIN.

While traveling with Mr. P.N. Nair, in India, I was most fortunate to visit Kanyakumari (Cape Comorin), where the Arabian Sea and the Bay of Bengal meld into the Indian Ocean. It is a pilgrimage destination of great spiritual significance to Hindus. A memorial to Swami Vivekananda, the Indian philosopher and crusader, is located there. Also located in Kanyakumari, is Gandhi Mandapam, the temporary place where the cremated remains of Mahatma Gandhi were kept in the year before immersion. The memorial on the next page shows the exact spot where the cremains were held, and, the writing above, in Gandhi's own words, tells the reason why he chose the Cape.

About the Authors

Margaret A. Goralski has co-authored A Passbook to India with Murale Gopinathan and has written monthly columns in Middlesex Business Review and New England Real Estate Journal.

Ellen Rusconi-Black is Vice President of Marketing at Kuhn Employment Opportunities, Inc. in Meriden, Connecticut.

Robert B. Bailey is the third generation owner and operator of the B. C. Bailey Funeral Home in Wallingford, Connecticut. His grandfather, C. W. Bailey, founded the Funeral Home.

Index

9 780595 139743